BALACHANDRAN VISWARAM is a full-time options trader and a blogging enthusiast. He writes on investing, concepts in trading and unique strategies using mutual funds.

Before becoming a trader, he was in the IT sector and even tried his luck as an entrepreneur. He has written on options trading and is also a guest columnist for Sampadyam by Malayala Manorama.

Balachandran is an NISM certified Research Analyst, Investment Adviser L1 and MFD. He is also a student of MA in Economics. He is happily married with three children, and lives in Kochi, Kerala. He can be reached at balu@viswaram.com.

HOW TO JOIN THE TOP 1% OPTIONS TRADERS CLUB

FROM STARTING OUT TO PROFITABLE TRADING

BALACHANDRAN VISWARAM

VISION BOOKS

www.visionbooksindia.com

www.visionbooksindia.com

Disclaimer

Investing and trading invariably involve some risk. The author and the publisher disclaim all legal or other responsibilities for any losses which readers may suffer by investing or trading based on information provided in this book, which is meant only for educational purpose. Readers are advised to seek professional advice and guidance before making any trades or investments.

A Vision Books Original

ISBN 10: 81-947275-9-6
ISBN 13: 978-81-947275-9-0

First Published in 2025 by
Vision Books Pvt. Ltd.
(Incorporating Orient Paperbacks and CARING imprints)
24 Feroze Gandhi Road, Lajpat Nagar 3
New Delhi 110024, India.
Phone: (+91-11) 2984 0821 / 22
e-mail: visionbooks@gmail.com

Printed at
Ashim Print Line
38/2, 35 & 36 Sahibabad Industrial Area, Ghaziabad
Uttar Pradesh 201010, India

Contents

Section 2

Section 3

Section 4

Preface

What This Book Offers You

IF YOU TRADE OR INVEST IN STOCKS, you might have heard of Nithin Kamath, co-founder of Zerodha. The inspiration to write this book is from his article published in *The Economic Times* on 3 January 2022 in which Nithin is quoted as saying, **". . . the reality is (that only) less than 1% of active traders earn more money than a bank fixed deposit over a 3-year period."**

This statement shook me to the core. Popular narrative would have you believe that of all the investment opportunities available, stock market trading should be the easiest place to make money. Yet, 99% of the participants can't even beat the return available from a fixed deposit!

Not just that.

India's financial markets watchdog SEBI published a report* of its findings about how many people actually profit from trading (*see* Figure 0.1). Some important highlights:

1. During FY22, (only) **11% of individual traders in equity futures and options (F&O) segment made profit with an average profit of ₹1.5 lakh**.

---

* You can read the full document at: https://www.sebi.gov.in/reports-and-statistics/research/jan-2023/study-analysis-of-profit-and-loss-of-individual-traders-dealing-in-equity-fando-segment_67525.html.

The percentage went down marginally to 10% for active traders, though the average profit made by them went up to ₹1.9 lakh during the same period.

2. From among the group of active traders, excluding a few outliers, only **6% of individual traders in equity F&O segment made profit,** the average profit being nearly ₹3,400 in FY22.
3. The **top 1% and top 5% active profit makers** accounted for nearly 51% and 75% of the total net profit earned by all active profit makers, respectively.

Loss Makers

- 89% of the individual traders (i.e. 9 out of 10 individual traders) in equity F&O segment incurred losses, with an average loss of ₹1.1 lakh during FY22, whereas, 90% of the active traders incurred average losses of ₹1.25 lakh during the same period.
- For the group of active traders (excluding outliers), on average, loss makers registered not trading loss close to ₹50,000 in FY22.
- For the group of active traders (excluding outliers), the average loss of a loss maker was over 15 times the average profit by a profit maker during FY22.

Profit Makers

- During FY22, 11% of individual traders in equity F&O segment made profit with an average profit of ₹1.5 lakhs. The percentage went down marginally to 10% for active traders, though the average profit made by them went up to ₹1.9 lakh during the same period.
- For the group of active traders (excluding outliers), only 6% of individual traders in equity F&O segment made profit with an average profit of nearly ₹3,400 in FY22.
- The top 1 percent and top 5 percent active profit markers accounted for nearly 51% and 75% of the total net profit earned by all active profit makers, respectively.

Figure 0.1: **Highlight of SEBI's Research Report**

Table 0.1

Summary Statistics of P&L of Active Individual Traders

	₹ Crore	
	FY19	*FY22*
Average P&L	-81,608	-56,758
Median P&L	-30,576	-21,768
25th percentile P&L	-1,01,563	-69,489
% of individual traders who made losses	91%	94%
% of individual traders who made profit	9%	6%
Average profit made by profit makers	8,347	3,365
Average loss made by loss makers	-90,691	-60,314
Average net trading profit made by profit makers	15,989	7,030
Average net trading loss made by loss makers	-68,469	-46,969

4. During FY22, **89% of individuals** who traded in index options, and 82% of individual traders who traded in stock options incurred an **average loss** of ₹0.77 lakh and ₹0.66 lakh each, respectively. The percentage of loss makers were 74% and 67% for index futures and stock futures with an average loss of ₹0.96 lakh and ₹2.1 lakh, respectively.

   For the group of active traders, excluding outliers, 6% of individual traders in equity F&O segment made profit with an average profit of ₹3,365 in FY22 (*see* Table 0.1).

   The top 1% and top 5% active profit makers accounted for nearly 51% and 75% of the total net profit earned by all active profit makers, respectively.

The broader point or the big picture that emerges from SEBI's analysis is that only a small fraction of individual traders make profits.

This book is an attempt to investigate:

1. Is there a way you can be in the top 1% of profit-making traders?

2. Can you beat fixed deposit returns?

At the very outset, let us set out the expectations correctly. This book is NOT for those who are looking for:

1. Massive returns from stock markets.
2. Finding 1,000x multibaggers and holding them for life.
3. Strategies for making big money in stock markets.
4. Investing ₹1,000 in the expectation of making it into ₹1 crore in just a few years.
5. Insider tips and other shortcuts for making money.

Rather, this book is meant for those who are looking to:

1. Beat the bank fixed deposit returns every year.
2. Grow their capital consistently with minimal drawdowns.
3. Learn intermediate and advanced option strategies that will make you a profitable trader.

For the purposes of this book, I am assuming that you have little or no experience in the stock market, debt mutual funds or options trading. If you do have some experience, then I guess it is time to re-learn it the right way because most people who enter the trading profession look for a lottery-like success.

In other words, most individual traders tend to gamble with their money, thinking:

- I am okay even if I lose ₹10,000 on this XYZ stock.
- If the stock I buy goes down, I will hold it for the rest of my life.
- I'm buying on a tip from a friend expecting a 10-fold return in one to two months.
- Only if I sell the stock does it become a realized loss.

- The stock market is akin to gambling and I expect to hit a jackpot.

The hard truth is that none of the above statements is true. Stock trading is just another profession with a similar chance of success as there is in any other field. The fact that more people are entering trading with the mindset that "they are ready to lose money" makes it easier for the smarter trader to win the money off them.

This book is an effort to help you become a disciplined trader within three years. While I'm obviously happy that you're reading this book, but as you go through your trading journey you might require additional learning resources.

And in this three-year period you will gain insights into how the markets function.

Plus, you will earn as you learn.

You will beat FD returns for sure — 100% guaranteed. And after three years you can go further and try innovative strategies to make a living!

The pages ahead reflect what I did and learnt from the period from 27 March 2020 to 31 March 2023. During this period I became a full-time trader — not out of choice — but out of compulsion because the Covid lockdown bankrupted our family business.

I got a head-start with a seed capital that was saved *via* mutual funds right from 2007. The first, cardinal, rule I set for myself was not to lose this seed capital — so every trade I took was keeping this in mind.

Also, I had to meet my monthly expenses. So I started with a clear-cut goal — trades that could give me ₹500 per day. The biggest reason for things working out perfectly for me in the next three years was because my expectations were very realistic.

And since I kept a daily journal during this period it was easy to document and publish what I learnt — and so emerged this book.

In the pages ahead there will be statements such as, "I recommend you to . . .", "You should plan to . . .", etc. These are to be taken with an educational intent, not as recommendations.

This book is not about me; it is about you. You can learn from my years of planning, researching and trading so that you do not have to spend your next three years repeating my failures.

During this 3-year period, I must have read more than 50 books on trading, and also watched more than 800 videos. No single book or video offered me a complete structure or a step-by-step trading strategy. Most either explained the theory, or focused exclusively on trade execution. Thus, one would have to connect the dots and by oneself to figure out how those authors put the theory into execution.

This book is an attempt to address that issue. It first offers you detailed step-by-step instruction on the theory and, then, explains its execution. I hope this book will prepare you to survive the battlefield known as stock markets.

Come, let us get started.

BALACHANDRAN VISWARAM

Alert: I will be revising the book based on the comments and experiences of fellow traders. I am specifically interviewing only traders who underperformed the fixed deposit in a three-year period.

This will add more perspective to this subject and provide another angle to look at things.

List of Abbreviations

0DTE	Zero Day to Expiry.
ADX	Average Directional Index.
AI	Artificial Intelligence.
AMCs	Asset Management Companies.
AMFI	Association of Mutual Funds in India.
APIs	Application Programming Interface, i.e. access to connect the broker's system from a third party application, mainly for algorithmic trading.
ATM	At the Money.
ATR	Average True Range.
CDSL	Central Depository Services (India) Limited
CPU	Corporate Payment Undertaking
DICGC	Deposit Insurance and Credit Guarantee Corporation.
DMI	Directional Movement Index.
D-SIBs	Domestic Systemically Significant Banks.
ELM	Extreme Loss Margin.
EMA	Exponential Moving Average.
EMIs	Equated Monthly Instalments.
EPS	Earnings Per Share.
F&O	Future and Options
FDs	Fixed deposits.
GDP	Gross Domestic Product.
GOI	Government of India.

G-Secs	Government Securities.
HNIs	High Net Worth Individuals.
IM	Initial Margin.
IRDAI	Insurance Regulatory and Development Authority of India.
IT	Information Technology.
ITM	In the Money.
ISINs	International Securities Identification Numbers
LAC	Line of Actual Control.
LVB	Lakshmi Vilas Bank
MACD	Moving Average Convergence / Divergence.
MFD	Mutual Fund Distributor.
NBFCs	Non-Banking Financial Companies.
NII	Net interest income.
NISM	National Institute of Securities Markets.
NPA	Non Performing Asset.
NSDL	National Securities Depository Limited.
NSE	National Stock Exchange.
OTM	Out of the Money.
OTP	One time Password.
PEG ratio	Price / Earnings to Growth ratio.
PSU fund	Public Sector Undertaking fund
RAT	Research, Analyze and Test Cycle
RBI	Reserve Bank of India.
ROI	Return on Investment.
RSI	Relative Strength Index.
SBI	State Bank of India.
SCORES	SEBI Complaints Redress System (SCORES is an online grievance redressal facilitation platform provided by SEBI)
SEBI	Securities and Exchange Board of India.
SIP	Systematic Investment Plans.
SPAN	Standard Portfolio Analysis of Risk.
TREPS	Treasury Bills Repurchase.
QoQ	Quarter on Quarter.
YoY	Year Over Year.

Section

~

1

1

~

Understanding Fixed Deposits

A THOROUGH AND CLEAR UNDERSTANDING of fixed deposits (FDs) and other debt instruments is crucial in our journey. Only if we know FDs in and out, will we be able to design a strategy to outperform them.

The number one reason most stock traders are not able to beat the quite humble returns available from fixed deposits is that their expectation is way beyond their financial knowledge. Approaching the stock markets with the hope of generating 100% returns in one year, for example, reveals utterly wrong expectations based on poor financial knowledge. But setting a modest target of 7% returns a year — may not sound worth their time.

So, what do you think should be a fair return on investment (ROI) from stock markets every year?

Some of us may be engineers, doctors, lawyers, teachers, bankers or IT employees. And we may be smart performers at our work place. But that does not mean one is also financially smart.

The root cause of financial illiteracy begins from school. We learn advanced calculus, geometry, statistics and physics, chemistry, etc., many of which have no real applications in our day-to-day lives. On the other hand, nobody teaches us how money is earned, how the economy functions, or how equity markets work. We are not even taught the basics of supply and demand.

Then you get into a high paying job which provides you disposable salary. The first thing your friends then suggest is that "you can double your money in stock markets." Many would definitely fall for it. This creates a betting psychology, or a lottery mindset. People approach stock markets as an arena to gamble in and win big. Typically, instead, they lose what they had.

This book will show you an alternate path; the path to create wealth by first earning your financial literacy degree. Fixed deposits will form the foundation of our options trading strategy, and in chapters 8 to 10 we will discuss how to build many more floors atop this foundation. The book also offers real-life examples, charts and comparisons so that you can learn these the right way. And as your financial knowledge increases, you will then be able to soon build a skyscraper.

I have seen my friends do hours of research before buying their next smartphone, but just a few minutes, if that, to buy a stock.

The fixed deposit is the best known and the most popular investment instrument in India. That is because we all know someone or the other who works at a local bank and who persuaded, almost forced, us to book an FD to meet their monthly targets. This neighbor, relative or friend would be someone to whom we could not say no. Most often their targets are our parents or grand-parents who are much more soft-hearted than us.

Once we start receiving interest from the FD, whether it be monthly, quarterly, or yearly, we feel proud and satisfied about our investment decision — and at seeing our money grow. The respect for that person who "pushed us" into FDs would also go up, whereupon we may sometimes end up investing into even more FDs.

Fixed deposits are simple to understand. You receive interest every month, every quarter or annually as opted by you. This simplicity and predictability of receiving regular interest payment is what make FDs appealing to the public at large, and especially older people. At the end of the period anyone can accurately calculate how much money you are going to receive.

There are two types of income that every investor aims for:

1. Rental income; and
2. Interest income.

Both these are called fixed incomes, insofar as they are time-predictable and also amount-predictable.

Rental income is something we get when we let out our residential or commercial property to a tenant. The tenant pays the agreed upon rent every month and this is akin to an assured income for the contracted period.

Interest income is what the banks give you when you open a fixed deposit with them. As long as you maintain the deposit, you will keep receiving the interest income.

Generating rental income is quite an uphill task when one is just starting a career — because you first need to have a property which can then be let out. Acquiring such a property takes a sizeable amount of money. On the other hand, fixed deposit income is more easily obtained since one can save some money every month and keep putting it in the bank.

Let us focus on fixed deposits as it's the subject of our interest here. Banks usually serve two major purposes:

1. They lend money to people as loans; and
2. They accept money from people as deposits.

When banks lend money, they do so at a higher interest rate, let's say, at 10%, while they pay a lower interest on the deposits and FDs they accept from people, let's say 7%. The difference between interest rates on loans and deposits, called "spread" in banking lingo, is what is called the bank's net interest income (NII). That's also the profit that banks most commonly make.

So suppose you approach a bank to deposit ₹20 lakh of your money. The bank will typically have varying deposit rates based on the tenure of the deposit. In other words, the interest rate offered depends on the time period for which you commit the deposit.

As example, the interest rate table of three major Indian banks, SBI, HDFC Bank and ICICI Bank are shown in Figure 1.1, 1.2 and 1.3 respectively.

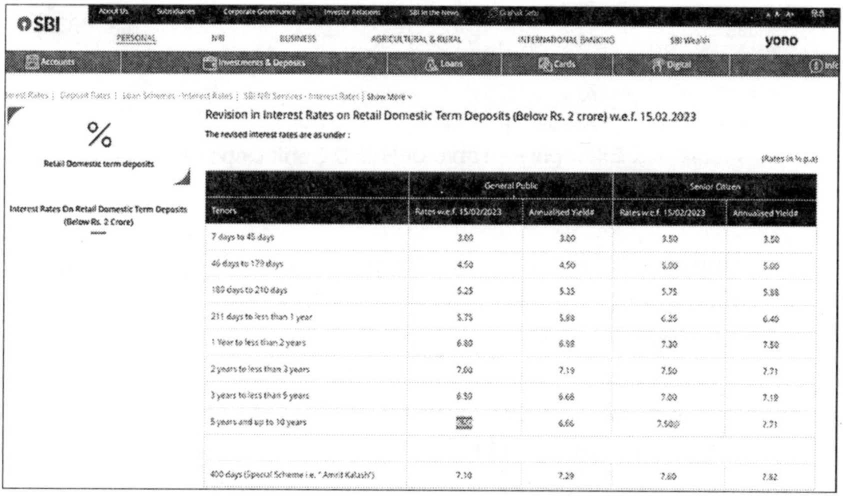

Revision in Interest Rates on Retail Domestic Term Deposits (Below Rs. 2 crore) w.e.f. 15.02.2023

The revised interest rates are as under :

(Rates in % p.a)

	General Public		Senior Citizen	
Tenors	Rates w.e.f. 15/02/2023	Annualised Yield#	Rates w.e.f. 15/02/2023	Annualised Yield#
7 days to 45 days	3.00	3.00	3.50	3.50
46 days to 179 days	4.50	4.50	5.00	5.00
180 days to 210 days	5.25	5.35	5.75	5.88
211 days to less than 1 year	5.75	5.88	6.25	6.40
1 Year to less than 2 years	6.80	6.98	7.30	7.50
2 years to less than 3 years	7.00	7.19	7.50	7.71
3 years to less than 5 years	6.50	6.68	7.00	7.19
5 years and up to 10 years	[illegible]	6.66	7.50@	7.71
400 days (Special Scheme i.e. "Amrit Kalash")	7.10	7.29	7.60	7.82

Figure 1.1: **Example — Table of SBI Deposit Rates**

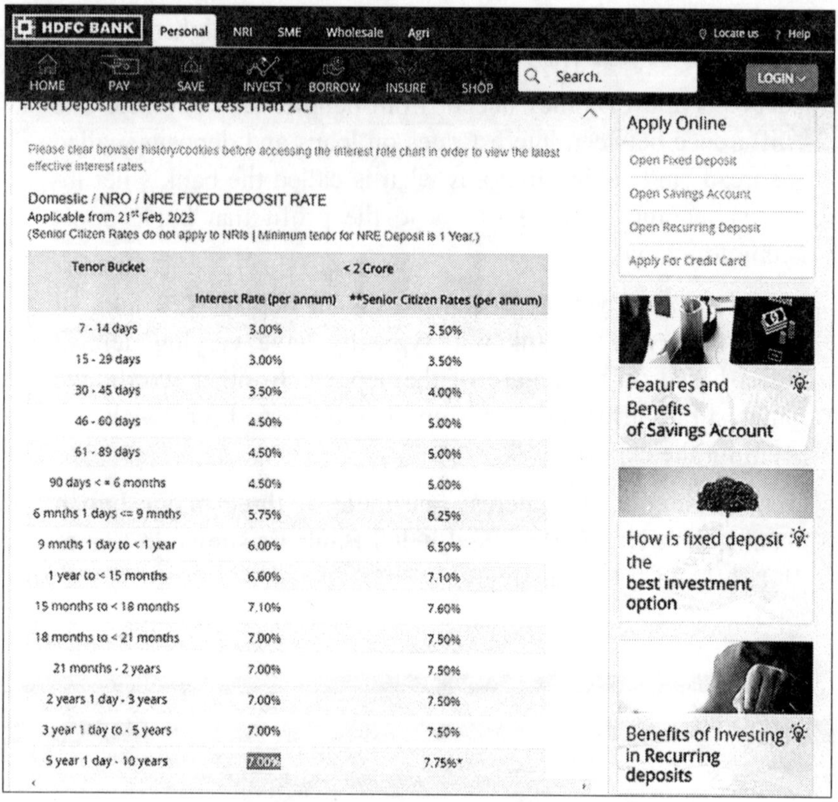

HDFC BANK | Personal | NRI | SME | Wholesale | Agri | Locate us | ? Help

HOME | PAY | SAVE | INVEST | BORROW | INSURE | SHOP | Search. | LOGIN

Fixed Deposit Interest Rate Less Than 2 Cr

Please clear browser history/cookies before accessing the interest rate chart in order to view the latest effective interest rates.

Domestic / NRO / NRE FIXED DEPOSIT RATE
Applicable from 21st Feb, 2023
(Senior Citizen Rates do not apply to NRIs | Minimum tenor for NRE Deposit is 1 Year.)

Tenor Bucket	< 2 Crore	
	Interest Rate (per annum)	**Senior Citizen Rates (per annum)
7 - 14 days	3.00%	3.50%
15 - 29 days	3.00%	3.50%
30 - 45 days	3.50%	4.00%
46 - 60 days	4.50%	5.00%
61 - 89 days	4.50%	5.00%
90 days < = 6 months	4.50%	5.00%
6 mnths 1 days <= 9 mnths	5.75%	6.25%
9 mnths 1 day to < 1 year	6.00%	6.50%
1 year to < 15 months	6.60%	7.10%
15 months to < 18 months	7.10%	7.60%
18 months to < 21 months	7.00%	7.50%
21 months - 2 years	7.00%	7.50%
2 years 1 day - 3 years	7.00%	7.50%
3 year 1 day to - 5 years	7.00%	7.50%
5 year 1 day - 10 years	7.00%	7.75%*

Apply Online
Open Fixed Deposit
Open Savings Account
Open Recurring Deposit
Apply For Credit Card

Features and Benefits of Savings Account

How is fixed deposit the best investment option

Benefits of Investing in Recurring deposits

Figure 1.2: **Example — Table of HDFC Bank Deposit Rates**

Assuming the tenure to be 10 years, we can see that SBI was then offering 6.5%, HDFC Bank 7%, and ICICI Bank 6.9% interest.

Let us assume you go with HDFC Bank. Your ₹20 lakh will then provide you an yearly interest income of ₹1.40 lakh, or a monthly income of ₹11,441 at 7% interest.

FD INTEREST RATES | FIXED DEPOSIT | FD CALCULATOR | BENEFITS | DOCUMENTS REQUIRED | FAQS | VIDEOS | MORE

FD Interest rates on Domestic, NRO & NRE deposits(Less than ₹5 Crore)

Maturity Period	Interest rates (per cent per annum) w.e.f. February 24, 2023 Single deposit of less than ₹20.0 million		Interest rates (per cent per annum) w.e.f. April 14, 2023 Single deposit of ₹20.0 mn & above but less than 50.0 mn	
	General	**Senior Citizen	General	**Senior Citizen
7 days to 14 days	3.00%	3.50%	4.75%	4.75%
15 days to 29 days	3.00%	3.50%	4.75%	4.75%
30 days to 45 days	3.50%	4.00%	5.50%	5.50%
46 days to 60 days	4.25%	4.75%	5.75%	5.75%
61 days to 90 days	4.50%	5.00%	6.00%	6.00%
91 days to 120 days	4.75%	5.25%	6.50%	6.50%
121 days to 150 days	4.75%	5.25%	6.50%	6.50%
151 days to 184 days	4.75%	5.25%	6.50%	6.50%
185 days to 210 days	5.75%	6.25%	6.60%	6.65%
211 days to 270 days	5.75%	6.25%	6.65%	6.65%
271 days to 289 days	6.00%	6.50%	6.75%	6.75%
290 days to less than 1 year	6.00%	6.50%	6.75%	6.75%
1 year to 389 days	6.70%	7.20%	7.25%	7.25%
390 days to < 15 months	6.70%	7.20%	7.25%	7.25%
15 months to < 18 months	7.10%	7.60%	7.15%	7.15%
18 months to 2 years	7.10%	7.60%	7.15%	7.15%
2 years 1 day to 3 years	7.00%	7.50%	7.00%	7.00%
3 years 1 day to 5 years	7.00%	7.50%	6.75%	6.75%
5 years 1 day to 10 years	[illegible]	≥7.50%	6.75%	6.75%
5 Years (80C FD) – Max to `1.50 lac	7.00%	7.50%	NA	NA

Figure 1.3: **Example — Table of ICICI Bank Deposit Rates**

Not bad, right? Going forward we will focus on other investment instruments that give us a monthly income, just like the fixed deposit example here. This monthly income will even help you begin stock trading as a full-time career!

Please note, all the examples quoted in this book are based on an initial capital assumption of ₹20 lakh.

If we start with a lower capital, the returns would generally be proportional but we may incur higher transaction charges and brokerages. Most brokers these days have a fixed per order brokerage, e.g. ₹20 per order. In other words, whether you trade with 1 lot or 10 lots you will end up paying ₹20 per order. Of course, the economy of scale works better if you trade more lots per order. If you do not have this initial capital of

₹20 lakh, you need to take up a job or business that will help you accumulate this capital. The stock market is not a magical place to make something out of nothing.

Like in any other traditional business, even in the stock market you need money in order to make money. You need to have an initial capital, some running capital, and also some funds saved away for rainy days, i.e. an emergency fund.

~

I will explain why a ₹20 lakh starting capital is required. Suppose you get a 7% return, it translates into ₹1.4 lakh per year, or nearly ₹11,667 per month. Suppose your initial capital is only ₹5 lakh, the interest income you will get per month will be only ₹2,916. This small amount will hardly pay even your internet and mobile monthly bills/EMI!

Also, the amount of ₹2,900 per month amount is quite unlikely to inspire you to take up trading as a full-time job. Try convincing your spouse, family or girl-friend that you are making ₹2,900 a month and see the reaction!

Okay, now if that did not discourage you and you are still passionate enough to become a successful trader — let me give you an alternate approach. Suppose you have a low initial capital of, say, ₹5 lakh instead of the recommended ₹20 lakh and yet want to become a disciplined, profitable trader. Then in all the examples in the chapters to follow apply the ratio 5:20, i.e. 1:4.

Take smaller positions which align with the lower capital. The amount of money you make will be lower, but percentage wise the profit would be the same.

Recent SEBI pronouncements point to increasing contract sizes of options and futures. This simply means that people with a low initial capital may find it hard to trade these instruments. You would be able to trade with ₹5 lakh right now, but the contract value may go up in the future, and when it does you may not be able to continue trading if the minimum capital requirements are not met.

Keep in mind, however, that the transaction charges as a percentage of returns earned will really eat you alive when you trade with lower capital. That is because at the time of this brokers like Zerodha charge ₹20 per order, whether the order size is ₹5 lakh or ₹20 lakh.

YouTube is flooded with influencers claiming you can make ₹10,000 to ₹1 crore per year through stock market trading. If you feel this makes sense — then I very much doubt that this book will do you any good.

~

Now we need to know how fixed deposits work. It may seem a boring topic but let us try and grasp the important basic ideas that will form the foundation for our journey ahead.

As per HDFC Bank, "A fixed deposit is an account opened with a bank wherein, the bank pays a guaranteed interest rate on the sums deposited in a fixed deposit account, for a stipulated period or tenure." Creating a fixed deposit allows you to earn higher returns on funds lying idle in your savings account.

Banks provide both savings account and current account facilities, the latter used mainly by businesses, and depositors of these accounts can withdraw their money at any time. Current accounts have no minimum balance requirements either, which means that banks can't be certain, nor accurately estimate, how much total money the bank might have at any time. Banks, however, require a reasonable estimate of the deposits they have in order to ascertain the amount of funds they can give out as loans. The best way for them to raise these funds is by attracting fixed deposits.

In a fixed deposit, the bank blocks the money deposited for the duration of the deposit period. Banks allow depositors the flexibility to create fixed deposits for tenures (periods) from as low as seven days to as long as up to ten years. The interest rate you earn on the deposit depends on the period for which you placed funds with the bank.

The depositor is generally not allowed to withdraw the money deposited before the due date. Some banks do offer premature withdrawal facilities, but premature withdrawal comes with the penalty of a lower interest rate. On the maturity date, the bank credits the principal and interest to the depositor's bank account.

Thus, if you choose to create an FD, you should know the interest, tenure, and other key terms of the offering before locking away your funds for the stipulated period. You can also calculate the FD amount and the interest you will earn, using the FD calculator to help you make an informed decision.

Now the money you deposit for your chosen tenure is, in turn, used by the bank in issuing loans to other customers. If you wish to know the basics then I suggest you read *Central Banking 101* by Joseph J Wang.

So the money you deposit as FD enables banks to issue loans. They do this using the concept called as "fractional reserve banking".

If we go by the above example, the bank will not lend the entire ₹20 lakh to just any one person, or any one company. They would split it up among a number of borrowers. And the chances that all of them not being able to repay the loan, or default, is quite rare.

The important learning here is that a bank will not collapse even if two or three big corporates, or HNIs, default. As per *Business Standard (20 December 2022)*,

> "As of March, top 50 willful defaulters in India owed ₹92,570 crore to the banks, Minister of state for finance Bhagwat Karad told the Lok Sabha on Monday. At ₹7,848 crore, Gitanjali Gems, founded by now-fugitive businessman Mehul Choksi, was the biggest defaulter.
>
> "Era Infra Engineering (₹5,879 crore), Rei Agro (₹4,803 crore), Concast Steel and Power (₹4,596 crore), ABG Shipyard (₹3,708 crore), Frost International (₹3,311 crore), Winsome Diamonds and Jewelry (₹2,931 crore), Rotomac Global (₹2,893 crore), Coastal Projects (₹2,311 crore) and Zoom Developers (₹2,147 crore) are the other big willful defaulters."*

Banks have systems in place to cover these risks. You might think that a ₹7,848 crore default is a huge number and the issuing bank would have collapsed. The truth is this loan might only have been less than 0.05% of the bank's total loan portfolio.

A bank can collapse only if a very large number of small individual borrowers, people like us, default, and not just one or two people. For that to happen there should be an unnatural event, such as a war, a major calamity, or an event like Covid, which happens say once in fifty years. Such disastrous events displace people, close down their businesses or puts them out of job. These people will, of course, be unable to repay the loans!

---

* "Top 50 willful defaulters in India owe ₹92,570 crore to banks: MoS Karad BS" Web Team New Delhi As of March, top 50 willful defaulters in India owed ₹92,570 crore to the banks, Minister of...www.business-standard.com

2

~

Are Fixed Deposits Really Safe?

TOWARDS THE END of the previous chapter, we discussed how a bank could collapse if the majority of its borrowers chose not to, or are unable to, pay back the money they borrow.

Usually that does not happen without an external trigger. Has that happened in the past — absolutely yes!

Could it happen in the future — yes, absolutely! That's because the basic human instinct of greed will never die!

As per *Business Insider (18 November 2020)**:

> "Over the last two years, India has seen other legacy names like IL&FS, DHFL, Yes Bank and PMC Bank go under.
>
> "Lakshmi Vilas Bank is the fifth financial firm to collapse in India within the last 30 months after IL&FS, DHFL," Yes . . . .

And then there are the countless small thrift societies, lenders and chit schemes that have collapsed without making headlines. In all such cases, countless people have lost their entire life savings due to reasons and events beyond their control.

---

* www.businessinsider.in

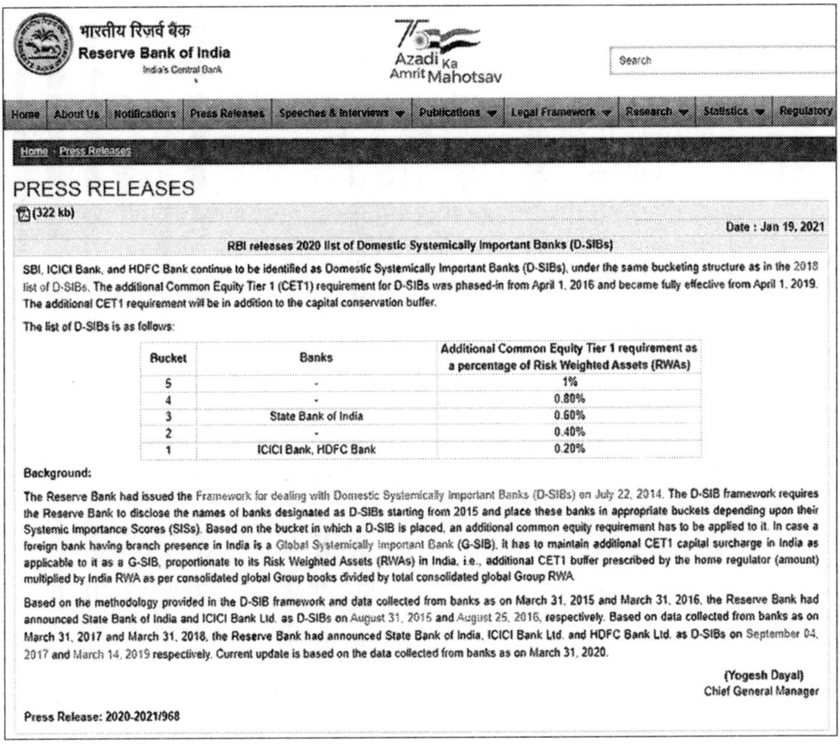

भारतीय रिज़र्व बैंक
Reserve Bank of India
India's Central Bank

Azadi Ka Amrit Mahotsav

Search

Home | About Us | Notifications | Press Releases | Speeches & Interviews | Publications | Legal Framework | Research | Statistics | Regulatory

Home · Press Releases

PRESS RELEASES

(322 kb)

Date : Jan 19, 2021

RBI releases 2020 list of Domestic Systemically Important Banks (D-SIBs)

SBI, ICICI Bank, and HDFC Bank continue to be identified as Domestic Systemically Important Banks (D-SIBs), under the same bucketing structure as in the 2018 list of D-SIBs. The additional Common Equity Tier 1 (CET1) requirement for D-SIBs was phased-in from April 1, 2016 and became fully effective from April 1, 2019. The additional CET1 requirement will be in addition to the capital conservation buffer.

The list of D-SIBs is as follows:

Bucket	Banks	Additional Common Equity Tier 1 requirement as a percentage of Risk Weighted Assets (RWAs)
5	-	1%
4	-	0.80%
3	State Bank of India	0.60%
2	-	0.40%
1	ICICI Bank, HDFC Bank	0.20%

Background:

The Reserve Bank had issued the Framework for dealing with Domestic Systemically Important Banks (D-SIBs) on July 22, 2014. The D-SIB framework requires the Reserve Bank to disclose the names of banks designated as D-SIBs starting from 2015 and place these banks in appropriate buckets depending upon their Systemic Importance Scores (SISs). Based on the bucket in which a D-SIB is placed, an additional common equity requirement has to be applied to it. In case a foreign bank having branch presence in India is a Global Systemically Important Bank (G-SIB), it has to maintain additional CET1 capital surcharge in India as applicable to it as a G-SIB, proportionate to its Risk Weighted Assets (RWAs) in India, i.e., additional CET1 buffer prescribed by the home regulator (amount) multiplied by India RWA as per consolidated global Group books divided by total consolidated global Group RWA.

Based on the methodology provided in the D-SIB framework and data collected from banks as on March 31, 2015 and March 31, 2016, the Reserve Bank had announced State Bank of India and ICICI Bank Ltd. as D-SIBs on August 31, 2015 and August 25, 2016, respectively. Based on data collected from banks as on March 31, 2017 and March 31, 2018, the Reserve Bank had announced State Bank of India, ICICI Bank Ltd. and HDFC Bank Ltd. as D-SIBs on September 04, 2017 and March 14, 2019 respectively. Current update is based on the data collected from banks as on March 31, 2020.

(Yogesh Dayal)
Chief General Manager

Press Release: 2020-2021/968

Figure 2.1:-**RBI D-SIB Classified Banks, 2021**

I strongly recommend you to consider parking your money only with "Domestic Systemically Significant Banks (D-SIBs)" banks as identified by the RBI. At the time of writing, there are three banks that are classified as D-SIBs. These are SBI, HDFC Bank and ICICI Bank (*see* Figure 2.1). What this means is that RBI or the Government of India would never let these three banks fail.

The fact is that the maximum amount that is insured by DICGC is ₹5 lakh.* So if you are really worried you could split your ₹20 lakh among the top 4 banks of India — ₹5 lakh in each bank. By doing so, even in the worst case you do not lose even a paisa!

Now, does all this mean that I am suggesting you to open a fixed deposit? Absolutely not. There are better debt instruments than FDs — and we will come to that. Do not make any investment decision before you complete reading this book.

Fixed deposit is just a start; it is the easiest one to understand among debt instruments. There are many other financial instruments safer and better than FDs and we will explore these in some detail.

Before getting into those other available debt instruments, however, let us just summarize the pros and cons of fixed deposits.

As per Bank of Baroda:

Advantages

1. **Assured rate of return:** The major reason why people prefer investing their funds in a fixed deposit is the assured rate of return these offer. Once you invest your funds in a fixed deposit account, you are guaranteed to receive the stated rate of return. Banks publish the fixed deposit rate of interest on their websites and in bank branches which makes it easy for a customer to ascertain how much return he will get. Banks also have a fixed deposit interest calculator on their websites where a customer can calculate the interest

* (https://www.dicgc.org.in/pdf/2023/PublicAwarenessMaterial/PosterOn-DepositorsProtection.pdf)

he will receive on investing a particular sum of money for a particular period.

2. **Tax threshold for interest:** Banks are not mandated to deduct tax on any interest until it crosses ₹10,000. This means that unless the total interest earned by a customer on all his / her fixed deposits tops ₹10,000, the bank will not deduct any tax. This provides comfort to small deposit holders.
3. **Flexible tenure:** The tenure for a fixed deposit is flexible and depends on the deposit holder. Each bank has their own minimum tenure rules; however, the final decision can be taken by the deposit holder. It is also possible to decide whether to redeem the fixed deposit or to extend it for the same period.
4. **Easy liquidation:** It is relatively easy to liquidate a fixed deposit. FDs booked online can be liquidated online *via* net banking as well. Most bank branches also have a form to liquidate the FD.
5. **Loans against fixed deposit:** An FD is a dependable instrument in case of financial emergencies. Taking a loan against a fixed deposit is very easy. You can obtain loan of up to 95% of the fixed deposit amount depending on the bank. This makes it a dependable investment.

Disadvantages

1. **Lower interest rates:** Even though fixed deposits have a lot of advantages; the interest rates do not move in line with inflation. This means in some cases you may actually earn less than the inflation rate. During periods when interest rates for fixed deposits are falling the attractiveness of this investment declines.
2. **Locked-in funds:** Fixed deposits lock in your funds for a fixed duration. These funds are not available for you to use unless

you withdraw the funds prematurely. Fixed deposits are not at all liquid and cannot be converted into cash easily.

3. **Penalties on premature withdrawal:** Banks charge a penalty from depositors who withdraw their fixed deposits prematurely. The penalty is in the form of a reduced rate of interest.
4. **No tax benefit:** The interest earned on fixed deposit is added to the deposit holder's taxable income. There is no tax deduction available on interest earned. However, senior citizens get a deduction up to ₹50,000 on interest.
5. **Fixed interest rate:** The rate of interest on a fixed deposit remains the same for the entire duration of the fixed deposit. Even if the rates increase in the interim for new fixed deposits, the bank does not pay additional interest to the existing deposit holder.

The real sad part of FDs is that the bulk of these deposits are parked with smaller finance compared, societies, chit funds or trusts. Most such organizations are not even under the RBI scanner. The reason why people do so is the higher return percentage offered.

One such firm to fold up in 2020 was "Popular Finance." The deposit rates they offered were 12% when the going bank rates were 5.9%.*

It is understandable why investors get tempted when being offered double the normal interest rate!

There are numerous other examples like this which may go unnoticed by the premier media, but which proved to be a killer of household savings!

* **Popular Finance fraud: Keralites lose millions to the ponzi scheme (04 Sep 2020)** The company, headquartered in remittance-fueled Pathanamthitta district, collected around ₹2,000 crore from thousands…www.livemint.com

3

~

Understanding Debt Funds

And, Are They Better than FDs?

HAVING UNDERSTOOD FIXED DEPOSITS, let's now review the world of debt instruments out there. This is the world of debt funds!

So, let's understand what debt funds are.

Let us assume Company XYZ is in the textile business with a business turnover of ₹5 crore in 2023. In 2024, it plans to further grow the business to ₹8 crore, and for doing so it requires an additional capital of ₹1 crore. The easiest place it can turn to for raising these funds is the bank with which the company has an account.

If not the banks where else could it get the funds from? That's where the debt market comes in.

Company XYZ could approach asset management companies (AMCs), HNIs or retail investors for its funding needs. Note, however, that since Company XYZ is not selling its stake to raise funds, so they can't raise money from the equity market.

This firm's next best option is to raise funds *via* debt financing. In this scenario, the firm will issue a "commercial paper", i.e. an agreement that it will pay a fixed amount of interest (monthly, quarterly, half-yearly or yearly) as per stipulated terms and conditions to the lender. In the example above, let us say Company XYZ raised the money *via* debt market rather than from banks. Of course, some banks like SBI, HDFC and ICICI also have their own asset management companies that provide such funding to big firms in India.

Almost all public or private companies require funding to run their businesses. The best place to raise money without diluting the existing equity holdings is the debt market. And these capital requirements could be as short as 7 days and go up to 30 years depending on the terms and conditions.

Debt funds are mutual funds handled by AMCs like SBI MF, HDFC MF, ICICI Prudential MF. They spread out and provide capital to multiple companies at the same time and thus reduce their NPA (non performing asset) risk.

These debt funds are important for us as we are going to choose these over the fixed deposits to give us a trading edge.

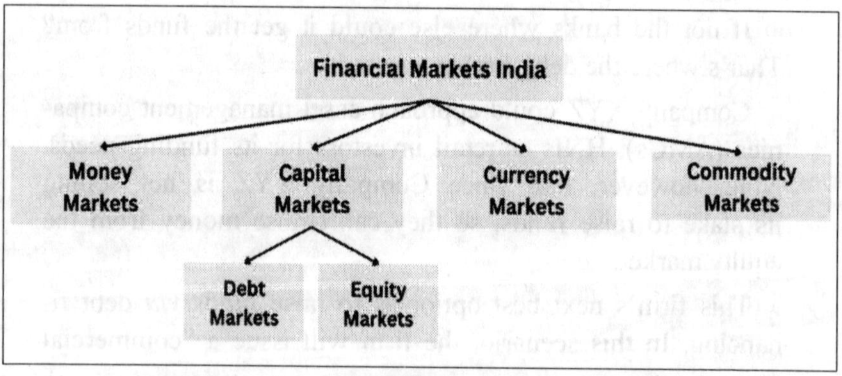

Figure 3.1: **Structure of Financial Markets in India**

Yes, that's correct. We will be selecting debt funds instead of fixed deposits. Even though we know that "99% of traders don't beat FD returns . . .", we would not be using FDs as a financial instrument as they are not pledgeable. Debt funds, and GOI bonds on the other hand can be kept as a collateral for margin funding.

We will be discussing the debt market as well as the money market. Both are similar in some ways, but also differ in many other.

Some of the available debt investment options are:

1. Liquid funds;
2. Overnight funds;
3. Banking & PSU funds;
4. Ultra short-term funds;
5. Dynamic bonds;
6. Corporate bonds;
7. Money market funds;
8. Gilt funds;
9. Floating rate funds;
10. Credit risk funds;
11. Short duration, medium duration and long duration funds;
12. GOI bonds / G-Secs funds of each type.

Each of the above categories can form a book in itself, but will not got into such details. To buy these funds you need a brokerage account as well as a demat account.

For this, I strongly suggest that you compare the various brokers operating in India and select the one you are most comfortable with. For the examples in this book, I would be quoting Zerodha, not just because it is the largest brokerage in India but also because I find their systems easy to understand and use.

There are two types of debt funds which we will specifically consider.

1. Funds that can be pledged with the broker as cash-equivalents.
2. Funds that belong to the non-cash category.

So, what is pledging? It is a system wherein you offer your investment as collateral and apply for a loan against it, or for obtaining permission to trade in the stock market.

Pledging might be a relatively new concept for you, and it might take you a while to fully understand it. But the richest 5% in the world widely use the collateral pledge to fund their capital requirements — and, also get tax breaks by doing so.

In our case we are exercising the right to trade with our own funds. More specifically, our funds are not held as cash, but invested in cash equivalent debt funds that continue to give us interest.

Zerodha categorizes the following types of funds in the cash-equivalent category:

1. Liquid funds;
2. Money market funds;
3. Overnight funds;
4. Gilt funds; and
5. GOI bonds.

We will look at these funds in some detail but first let's understand the two possible ways to handle the interest income that is generated:

1. Reinvestment of interest — called the growth option;
2. Interest payout at regular intervals, whether monthly, quarterly, half-yearly or yearly.

For the scope of this book, we will be considering the interest payout option. The rationale for doing so is that you may be just starting out in stock market trading and there may be a big doubt-cloud in front of you as to whether you would actually be able to make money regularly every month.

The receipt of regular interest will both calm you and give you something to fall back on when your trading may not do well. Once you become more proficient in trading you can revert to reinvestment of interest at any time.

More on this in Section 2.

Liquid Funds

When asset management companies invest in debt which has a maturity period of 3 months, or 91 days, then it is called a liquid fund. As an investor, you will be able to withdraw your capital from such funds on short notice; that's why the name "liquid". These funds do not have an exit load unless you withdraw your money within seven days of investing.

So before selecting a liquid fund, you need to pay heed to the exit load factor and also find out if there is any penalty for early redemption. Exit load is the fees charged by AMCs for premature redemption of mutual funds units.

Another factor to consider is the fund's expense ratio, which can be thought of as the charge you have to pay, as a percentage of your corpus in the fund, for managing your capital. Usually, the net returns you get is after deducting the expense ratio.

Let us look at an example.

SBI Liquid Fund: INF200K01UT4 growth
CAGR is the returns it gave in the 1-year period (May2022 to May 2023): 5.88%
Exit load: 0.007% till 7 days.
Expense ratio: 0.18%

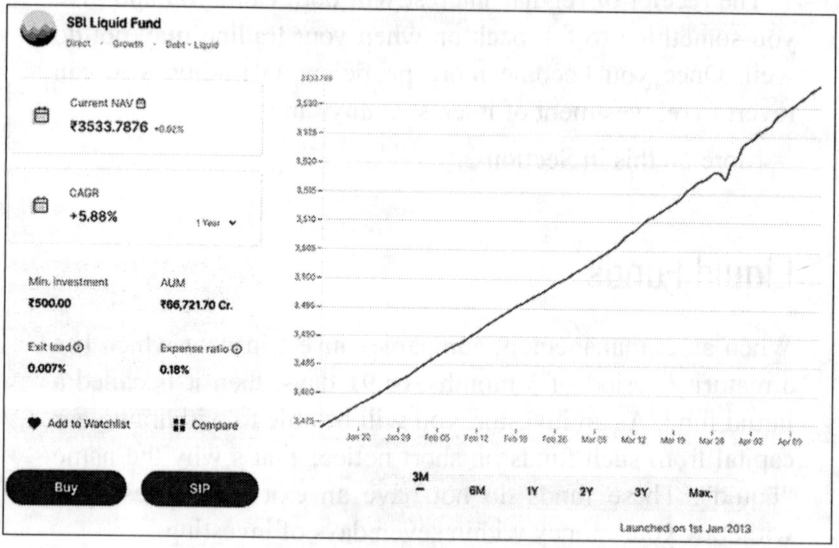

Figure 3.2: **SBI Liquid Fund Performance YoY**

Companies

Company	Allocation
TREPS	14.57%
91 DAY T-BILL 15.06.23	6.99%
National Bank for Agriculture and Rural Development	5.47%
Union Bank of India	5.15%
91 DAY T-BILL 08.06.23	4.87%
Punjab National Bank	4.44%
91 DAY T-BILL 20.04.23	3.84%
91 DAY T-BILL 01.06.23	3.73%
Reliance Retail Ventures Ltd.	2.99%
91 DAY T-BILL 23.03.23	2.99%
Small Industries Development Bank of India	2.96%
Bank of Maharashtra	2.95%
Bajaj Finance Ltd.	2.24%
Reliance Jio Infocomm Ltd.	2.22%
Bank of Maharashtra	2.21%
Canara Bank	2.19%

Figure 3.3: **Portfolio Allocation of SBI Mutual Fund**

As you can see from Figure 3.3. The top companies or institutions that have taken / borrowed funds from this AMC.

A liquid fund does not have the mandate to invest in equity; all its money will be invested in debt.

Money Market Funds

Money market funds have a close similarity with liquid funds, but the main difference comes in the quality of credit, i.e. a lower risk of going bust. The money market fund's liquidity is contributed by RBI, state governments, provident funds in addition to the AMCs, banks, NBFCs, corporates. Also funds are provided to the borrower for tenure lesser than 91 days. It could even be just one day.

Personally, I prefer money market debt funds a notch above liquid funds. Let us take the example of UTI money market fund: INF789F01XV6 growth.

Figure 3.4 depicts that UTI money mutual fund gave returns of 6.08% from May 2022 to May 2023. The exit load is 0%, during the one-year period and the expense ratio is 0.2%

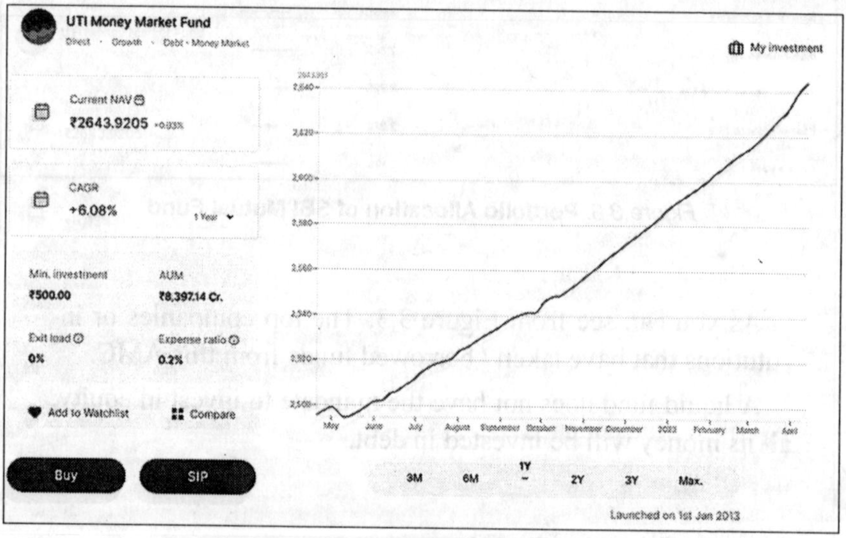

Figure 3.4: **UTI MF Performance YoY**

Companies

Company	Allocation
182 DAYS - 14/09/2023	6.90%
NET CURRENT ASSETS	6.48%
182 D TBILL MAT - 23/03/23	5.95%
SMALL INDST. DEV. BANK-30/05/23	3.52%
MAHINDRA & MAHINDRA FIN.SER.LTD.	2.88%
MOTILAL OSWAL FINANCIAL SERVICES LTD.	2.35%
HDFC BANK - 15/06/2023	2.34%
PANATONE FINVEST LTD.	2.34%
182 DAYS - 07/09/2023	2.30%
CANARA BANK - 04/12/2023	2.26%
ICICI BANK - 29/12/2023	2.25%
INDUSIND BANK - 19/01/2024	2.23%
HDFC LTD.	2.22%
TATA MOTORS FINANCE LTD.	2.08%
SMALL INDST. DEV. BANK-06/12/2023	1.97%
RELIANCE RETAIL VENTURES LIMITED	1.76%

Figure 3.5: **Portfolio Allocation of UTI Mutual Fund**

The percentage wise allocation of this fund is shown in Figure 3.5.

Overnight Funds

These are mutual funds that provide capital to borrowers for one day. It may appear strange but such funds do exist. The credit risk in such funds is extremely low because the chances of a borrower going bust in one day is naturally quite low — unless of course there is a nuclear explosion.

But the returns from these funds will be a notch lower than the liquid funds or money market funds. Consider the example of ICICI Prudential Overnight Fund: (INF109KC11G1 Growth) shown in Figure 3.6.

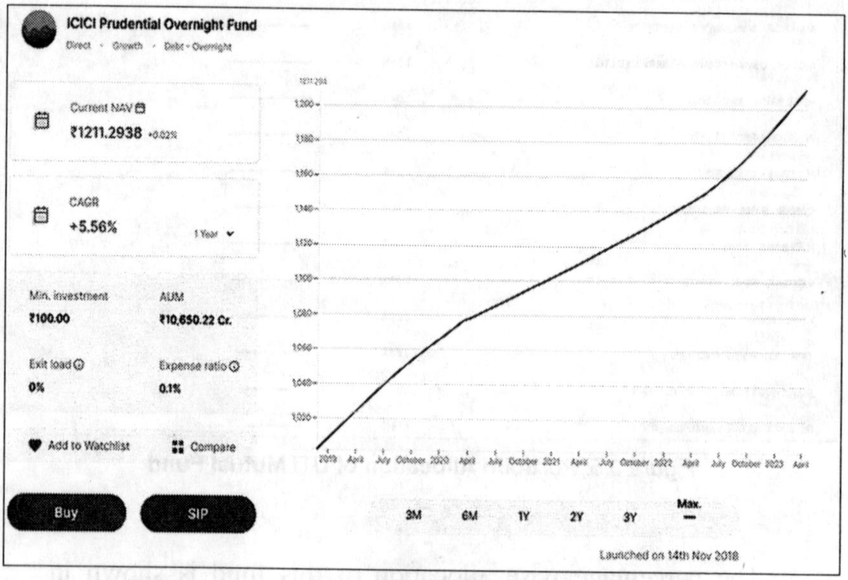

Figure 3.6: **ICICI Overnight Fund Performance YoY**

1-year. return = 5.56%;

Exit load = 0%;

Expense ratio: 0.1% lowest.

Companies

Company	Allocation
Reverse Repo	78.80%
Reverse Repo	62.80%
TREPS	33.75%
TREPS	14.84%
364 Days Treasury Bills	2.80%
91 Days Treasury Bills	1.40%
Net Current Assets	1.12%
182 Days Treasury Bills	1.00%
91 Days Treasury Bills	< 1%
182 Days Treasury Bills	< 1%
91 Days Treasury Bills	< 1%
182 Days Treasury Bills	< 1%
91 Days Treasury Bills	< 1%
Net Current Assets	< 1%
91 Days Treasury Bills	< 1%

Figure 3.7: **Portfolio Allocation of ICICI MF**

You can see most of the allocation was to Repo and T-bills, both of which are regulated by the RBI. The names of private sector are missing in the borrower's list.

Personally, I do not have any debt investments in overnight funds. One reason is the lower returns *vis-a-vis* money market or liquid funds. The other reason is that this category did not catch my interest when I started investing.

Gilt Funds

Mutual funds that invest only in government securities, T-bills or TREPS (Treasury Bills Repurchase) are known as Gilt fund; e.g. SBI Magnum Gilt Fund: (INF200K01SH3 Growth).

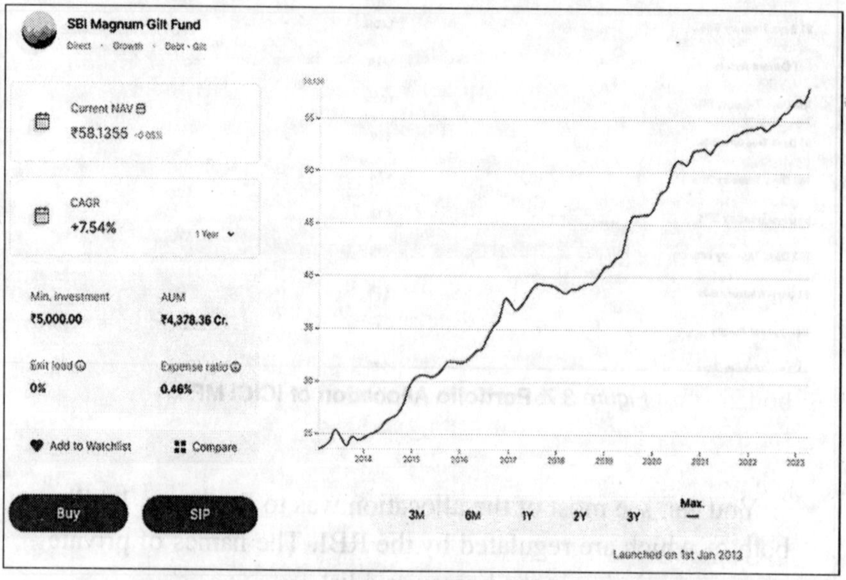

Figure 3.8: **SBI Magnum Gilt Fund Performance YoY**

1-year return = 7.54%;

Exit load = 0%;

Expense ratio = 0.46%.

Companies

Company	Allocation
7.38% CGL 2027	23.85%
7.10% CGL 2029	23.82%
TREPS	16.74%
7.26% CGL 2033	14.30%
7.40% CGL 2062	8.31%
364 DAY T-BILL 14.03.24	5.32%
7.26% CGL 2032	3.74%
7.36% CGL 2052	2.49%
7.54% CGL 2036	2.35%
Net Receivable/Payable	< 1%

Figure 3.9: **Portfolio Allocation of SBI MF**

As Figure 3.9 reveals, most of the allocation was into GOI bonds offering more than 7% interest. No wonder its return for the May 2022 to May 2023 period exceeded 7.54%.

GOI Bonds

We will discuss this topic in a separate chapter since this is the financial instrument we are going to consider for own initial three-years period. Remember, our first goal is to beat the FD returns in our initial a 3-year period.

To do that, we will invest in the most secure, zero failure risk GOI bonds which are backed by a sovereign guarantee. So long as the Government of India exists, it will honor the GOI bond's interest payments.

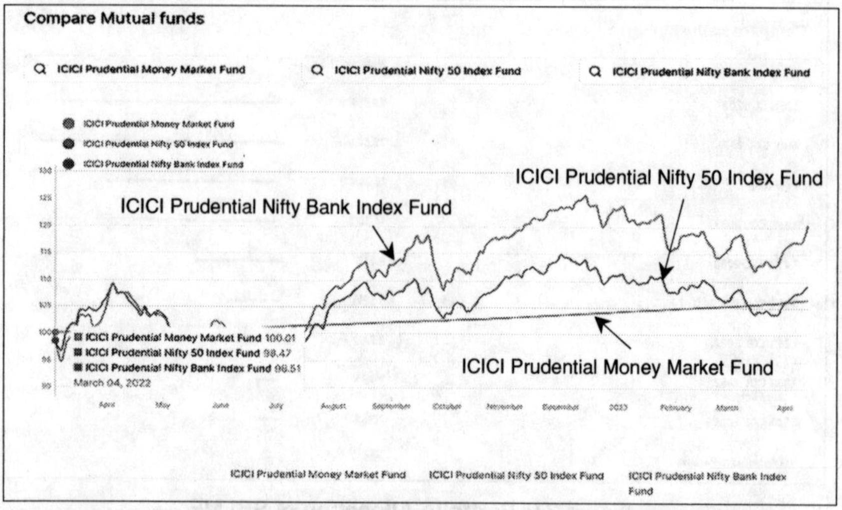

Figure 3.10: **Comparison of ICICI Money Market Fund, Nifty50 Index Fund, Niftybank Index Fund as on 2 March 2022**

Let us try to understand this with an example of ICICI Money Market Fund, Nifty50 Index Fund, Niftybank Index Fund (*see* Figure 3.10).

On 2 March 2022 each of them had the following values:

ICICI MMF: 100.01

ICICI Nifty50: 98.47

ICICI BankNifty: 98.51

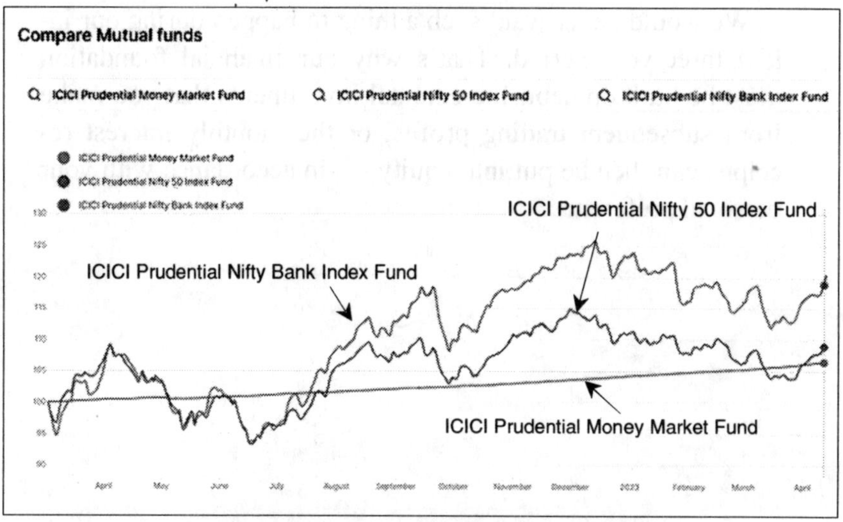

Figure 3.11: **Comparison of ICICI Money Market Fund, Nifty50 Index Fund, Niftybank Index Fund as on 12-04-2023**

And on 12 April 2023 these values became:

ICICI MMF: 106.47
ICICI Nifty50: 108.93
ICICI BankNifty: 118.85

As you can see from Figures 3.10 and 3.11, the debt fund's value increased slowly, whereas the equity fund rose and fell several times during each year. Also, there were four instances when the Nifty50 index underperformed a debt fund in this period.

Then, too, there were many months when the equity fund traded in negative territory, which means your capital would have been lower if you chose to withdraw your funds at such times.

We would never want such a thing to happen during our initial three-year period. That's why our financial foundation must be built on debt. Incremental investments that you make from subsequent trading profits, or the monthly interest receipts, can then be put into equity — in accordance with your personal preference.

4

~

Understanding Government of India (GOI) Bonds

THE REASON FOR THIS SEPARATE CHAPTER on GOI bonds underlines the significance of this financial instrument carries.

This is a relatively uncharted but a very important topic for the common investor

GOI bonds, a.k.a government securities, are issued by the Indian Government *via* Reserve Bank of India (RBI).

The government needs money to build roads, infrastructure, hospitals, etc. So it borrows money from the public *via* RBI which, in turn, raises the money by selling either bonds or T-bills through an auction, namely bidding, process.

What are GOI Bonds / T-bills?

Whenever you or I need money, we go to a bank and take a loan. Against this loan, we promise to pay the bank periodic interest and also return the borrowed money at the agreed upon time. This is usually how interest and borrowed principal are repaid to the bank.

Likewise, Government of India also needs money to build roads, bridges, dams, hospitals, etc. When it runs short of money, it approaches the country's central bank RBI for a loan. To raise funds for the government, RBI auctions bonds / T-bills to people at large.

Essentially, thus, you, I and many other Indians loan money to the government. Against this loan, Government of India promises to pay periodic interest, and also repay the principal at the end of the specified period.

The money which the government intends to repay within a year is borrowed *via* Treasury Bills, also commonly known as T-bills. Loans which the government intends to repay over many years are borrowed *via* bonds.

Our area of interest here are GOI bonds, and not T-bills. That's because T-bills cannot be pledged for trading; while GOI bonds are eligible.

Features of GOI Bonds

Here is what GOI bonds are:

1. It is the safest debt instrument in our country.
2. It is treated as a cash-equivalent by brokers.
3. It gives the highest interest rate yield.
4. We will select the most liquid of GOI bonds so that in the worst case if we have to redeem the bonds, we could do it at the lowest slippage possible.

Let us try to understand GOI bonds with an example (754GS2036-GS).

Just search for 754GS2036 in your broker's app. It is a 7.54% return yielding government security that has a tenure till 2036.

Let's assume you buy this bond at the face value with an initial investment of ₹20 lakh. This instrument will give you 7.54% returns, i.e. ₹1.508 lakh interest every year till 2036.

So in the subsequent 13 years you would have receive an interest of ₹19.604 lakh.

Now, there are two aspects to this scenario:

1. The interest payout is half-yearly; thus payouts will be on 23 November and 23 May every year.
2. It's quite impossible to buy this bond at its face value of ₹100 after its initial launch. At the time of this writing, for example, it was quoting at ₹104.60

So if you purchase this particular bond at ₹104.60 you will get a reduced yield of 7.21% till 2036, and incur a capital loss of ₹0.87952 lakh at the end of the bond's tenure.

So what would be the best time to buy this bond? It would have been between 22 to 24 May, or 22 to 24 November when a lot of investors were actually exiting from this bond.

The average prices at which I purchased this bond were between ₹101.50 to ₹102, but for that I had to wait for some time.

How do you calculate the yield? It is quite simple.

The face value of the bond is ₹100. So an investment of ₹20 lakh will buy you 20,000 units (2000000/100).

If the purchase price is ₹104.60, then you will get (2000000/104.60) 19120.458 units. It is not possible to own fractional units, so let us consider we got 19,120 units.

So the revised capital deployed is ₹19,99952 @ 104.60 per unit. Now, 19,120 units will offer you 7.54% annual interest totaling ₹1,44,164.80.

144164.8/1999952 in percentage = 7.21%.

What this means is that the closer the purchase price is to the ₹100 level, say if it is ₹101 or ₹102, it will offer you a better yield than if you buy this bond @ ₹104.60. A higher yield means you will get a higher amount as annual interest.

After the end of tenure you will have a capital loss of ₹87,952. That's because you have overpaid ₹4.60 per unit for the ₹100 face value bonds. (4.60 × 19120 = 87,952).

Now what happens if your purchase price is, say, ₹97?

In such a case, you will get 2000000/97 = 20,618.556 units. Let us round it off as 20,618 units.

So the revised capital deployed is ₹1999946 @ 97. These 20,618 units will offer you 7.54% annual interest, totaling ₹1,55,459.72.

155459.72/1999946 in percentage = 7.77%

Also you will have a capital gain of ₹3 x 20618 units, i.e. ₹61,854 at the end of bond's tenure.

Now, do the bonds ever actually trade below the face value of ₹100? Absolutely, yes, they do. To understand why you need to understand the interest rate cycle.

When the country is growing and its economic activity is at full steam, there is always the possibility that prices of various commodities, groceries, fuel, services might rise above their fair value. Such a situation is termed as inflation.

The rationale being that in a booming economy the employer is ready to pay higher wages to its employees. In turn, this employee is now ready to pay more money for the same product because he can afford it. This cycle continues.

Of course, when inflation gets very high it can kill the economy. Again, because the same employee might find it unaffordable if the prices of a particular commodity, say pulses, and exceed a threshold. If that commodity is an essential product, people will have to exhaust their savings to buy as the salary will not offset it.

A typical way in which central banks try to control inflation is to increase the interest rate. By doing so, the manufacturer will have to pay more interest on a new loan. This may prompt him to delay business expansion that is capital intensive. Sometimes he may have to shut down an existing part of the business in order to conserve capital.

To cut down costs he may even let go, or fire, a few employees. The fired employees will be unable to purchase many things as their earnings are now depleted.

So a fall in demand will quickly accompany the reduced supply created by a higher interest rate.

On the other hand, if the economy is in a poor shape, or in a recession, the central bank might decide to lower the interest rate. And, suddenly, the industry may find it viable to increase capacity, add more employees and produce more.

These are the inevitable boom and bust economic cycles, so are the interest rate cuts and hikes. You need not be a macroeconomic expert to gauge changes in the interest rate — but if you have this basic idea, you can plan your debt investments accordingly.

Essentially, bonds react inversely to interest rates. If interest rates are increasing, bonds will trade at a lower price. Similarly, when interest rates fall, bond prices will go up. ₹100 is the face value of a GOI bond. If the interest rates set by the RBI are going up, then the traded value of this bond will fall below ₹100, say ₹99 or ₹98, etc. On the other hand, if we are in a falling interest rate regime, the bond prices will go up, say ₹102, ₹103 etc.

I would strongly suggest that you to keep a close watch and buy only those GOI Bonds (G-Secs) that are actively traded every day. Trading liquidity is required if you wish to exit at a fair price.

~

	A	B	C	D	E	F	G	H	I
2	Yield calculator								
3									
4		Current trading price	Yield	Tenure	Amount you wish to purchase				
5	Input	97	7.54	2050	1999946			Capital Gain/Loss	61854
6								Overall interest Add/Sub	2209.071429
7								Final Yield	7.88%
8		base rate	number of units	effective yield	yearly interest amount	monthly interest			
9	Output	100	20618	7.77%	155459.72	12954.97667			
10									

Figure 4.1: **Example of Bond Yield Calculator**

~

I recommend that you pick up a G-Sec offering a good yield that can be pledged with your broker. Zerodha, for example, allows you to pledge G-Secs and it is in the cash component category.

I am not yet a SEBI approved research analyst. So, I am unable to offer you specific investment guidance. But to benefit from the book's suggestion, the first pre-condition you need to fulfil is owning a GOI bond that gives you interest payout.

If you are a trader and if you end up not generating even a single rupee profit in the 3-year span — you still end up winning. You are in the elite 1% because the returns from the G-Secs have matched the FD returns!

What you need to do is to avoid losing big, or losing your capital — more on that in Section 4.

~

Section

~

2

5

~

Starting with a Basic Debt Fund

IN THE PREVIOUS SECTION we discussed a few cash equivalent debt funds. While superficially all of them may seem similar, actually that's not the case. Each of the constituents of the debt classification has its pros and cons.

You would recollect our first suggestion was that you could park your ₹20 lakh into an interest-bearing instrument. There are two major styles of debt investment possible.

1. Growth; and
2. Payout of interest.

If you are familiar with the magic of compounding, you should definitely consider the growth option. In this option, the interest is not actually paid to you but is reinvested back on your behalf — and you start earning interest on interest.

Let us calculate what difference this interest on return makes over a 10-year period, based on a ₹20 lakh capital and at 7% interest rate.

With the growth option, you will have you total of ₹39.34 lakh at the end of 10 years, i.e. the original principal of ₹20 lakh, plus interest of ₹19.34 lakh (*see* Figure 5.1).

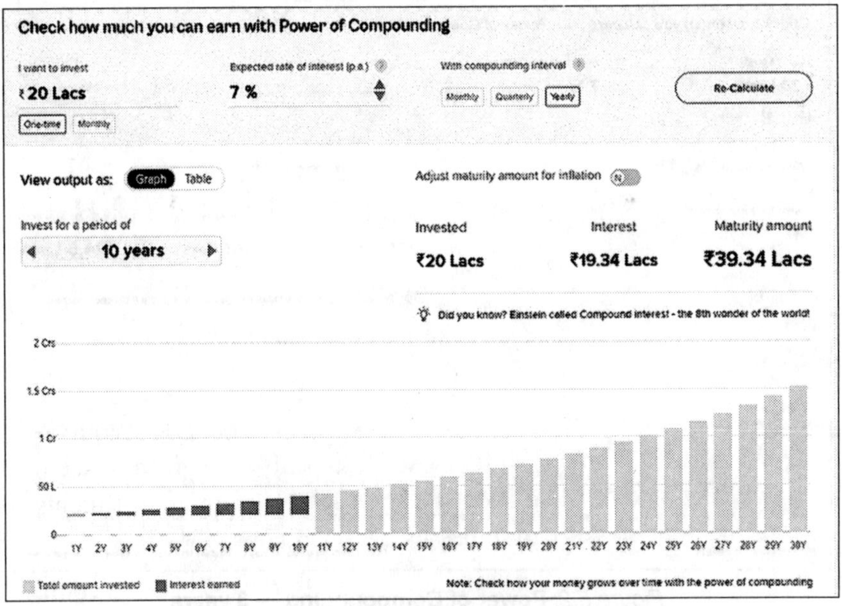

Figure 5.1: **Power of Compounding — 10 years**

Meanwhile if you select the interest payout option, i.e. 7% interest is paid out to you every year and you sum up the returns for 10 years.

7% interest on ₹20 lakh = ₹1.4 lakh per year.

Thus, over a 10-year period the total interest you would get is ₹14 lakh. So, the total of principal and interest after ten years is ₹34 lakh.

With this option, you miss out on ₹5.34 lakh of additional interest that you could have gained by opting for the growth option.

Let us now recalculate these options for the 3-year period. That's because we are here to become a full-time trader in 3 years!

Growth option: You get an interest of ₹4.5 lakh on ₹20 lakh.

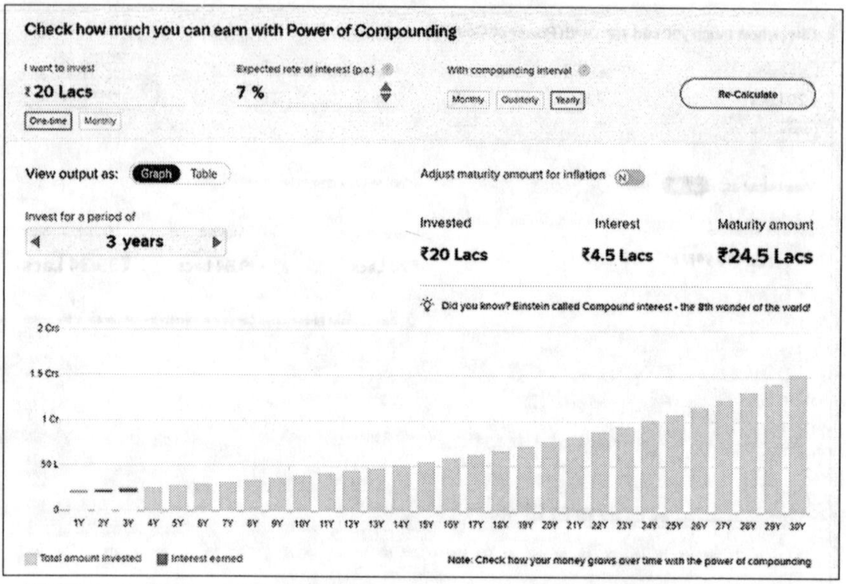

Figure 5.2: **Power of Compounding — 3 years**

Payout of interest option: You will get an interest of ₹4.2 lakh on ₹20 lakh. So the opportunity cost is just ₹30,000. That is something you can digest!

Why do I recommend the monthly or yearly payout of interest?

It is because setting up a trading business is very difficult, and expecting a regular return from it every month or every year is even more so. Which is why interest payout will give you some relief. And it will also give you enough courage to stay out of low profit trading setups / traps just to meet your income needs.

One thing is obvious — if you spend close to three years in any field, you will gather the required skills to be competent. I am not saying you will become the best trader in the world in three years. But I can say with confidence that you will be in the elite 5% group that makes profits from trading.

And after three years you can then rebalance your debt portfolio the way you want to. You need to have patience till then.

Alternately, you could act in accordance with your risk profile. You may split the allocation, e.g. 40% in growth and 60% in payout. Or 50:50, or 70:30 — it is all up to you.

The point is that though the magic of compounding is very powerful after, say 20 years, but at the outset that might seem a pretty long time.

Let us just look at the numbers once more.

In 20 years, the growth option will give you an interest of ₹57.39 lakh.

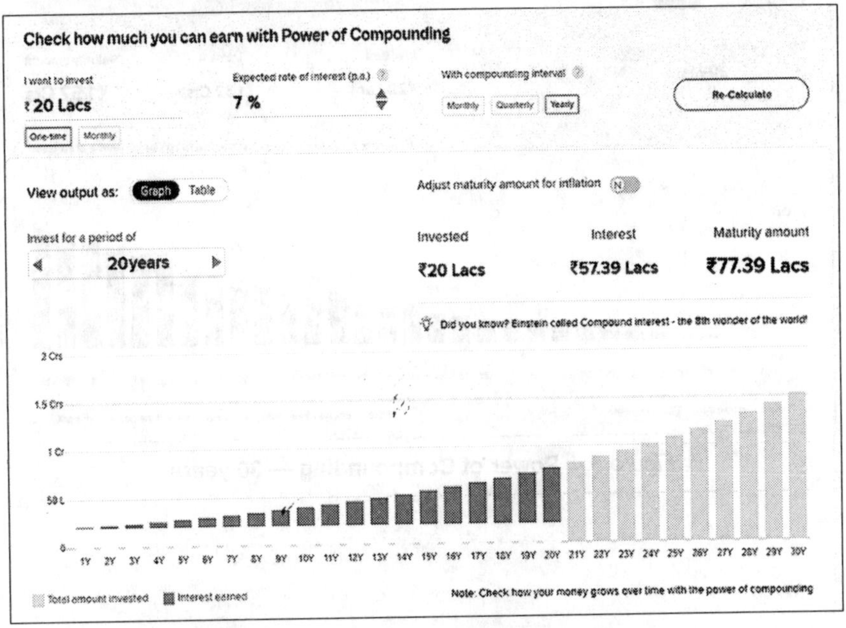

Figure 5.3: **Power of Compounding — 20 years**

The payout option will give you an interest of ₹28 lakh (1.40 × 20).

In other words, the magic of compounding will double your interest over a period of 20 years.

Let us now look at 30 years:

The growth option will give you an interest of: ₹1.32 crore ~ 132 lakh.

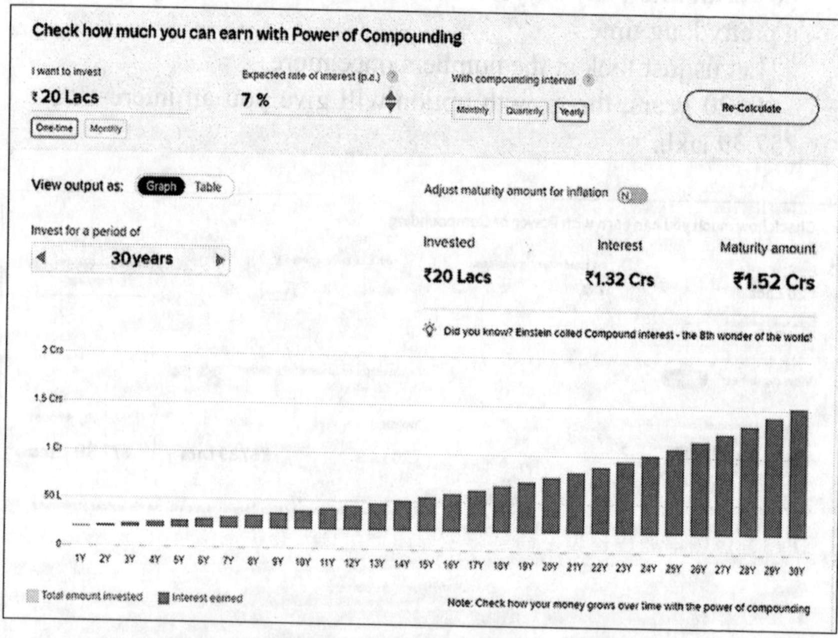

Figure 5.4: **Power of Compounding — 30 years**

The payout option will give you an interest of 1.40 × 30 = ₹42 lakh.

In other words, the growth option will give you three times higher returns *vis-à-vis* the payout option.

Real wealth is built over several years with the magic of compounding. It really does not look very significant during the first 3 years, but look at the difference the remaining 27 years make!

One thing that we have not yet factored in here is the tax impact. If you go in for the payout option, the income you receive is taxable and you get to retain a lower amount in your hand each year.

Let us say you are in the 30% tax slab. So out of the ₹1.40 lakh yearly payout income — you will get approximately only ₹0.98 lakh net in hand. So in a 30-year period you will get in hand ₹29.40 lakh of total interest income.

If you opt for the growth option, the taxation is only applicable on redemption, i.e. at the end of 30 years. Thus, you need to pay 30% tax on ₹1.32 crore, and you are left with ₹92.40 lakh as net income.

Taxation is something that you need to keep in mind for detailed calculation. But I am omitting this part to keep the numbers clean and simple.

~

I assume by now you have got the basic idea on how debt funds work and hope you are ready to deploy your capital.

The plan is to make 1% to 2% returns on your capital each month, safely and judiciously. That works out to ₹20,000 to ₹40,000 per month. This would appear quite a contrast to some YouTube finfluencers who say you could make 40% to 50% ROI per month. I am not saying that 40% to 50% monthly returns are impossible, but if you set your expectation that high — you could get into overtrading, lose your capital and end up miserable.

A pilot carrying 250 passengers, a specialized heart-surgeon, a civil engineer constructing a 100-floor building, a general commanding a fighting formation, and a stock market trader have one thing in common.

All of them are highly skilled and among the top 1% in their field. People might mislead you into thinking that the stock market is an easy place to make money — it is not. In fact, it is the toughest place there is.

6

~

How to Make Your Debt Fund Eligible for Trading

THIS IS THE CHAPTER THAT TURNS THE TIDE in your favor by meshing your debt funds with the trading plan.

Once you have invested ₹20 lakh in debt funds, the next step is to make those funds eligible for trading. The process by which you do so is called pledging. It is a process wherein you ask your broker to release funds for trading against your mutual funds or stock holdings. Conceptually, it is similar to taking a loan by pledging your land or gold as collateral. But in this specific case we are not taking funds out of our trading account, so there are no EMIs, payments or charges.

If you require a loan, the banks will usually ask you for a guarantee. This guarantee, namely collateral, is what you give over to the bank's custody till you are able to fully repay the loan. The banks give you loan with the confidence that even if you default — the collateral provided to the bank will cover its risk.

This collateral could be any anything — gold, bonds, land, house. Only tangible assets can be provided as collateral, i.e. items that have a high probability of value appreciation.

That is because the moment your repayment dues exceed the value of the collateral — you could choose to simply walk away from the asset you might have pledged to the bank. Banks would not want this to happen, so they will provide you a loan of only 60% to 75% of the asset's value.

For example, if your house is worth ₹50 lakh, and you approach a bank for loan valuation — the maximum they might offer would be ₹37 lakh to ₹38 lakh. The bank would wish to retain a buffer of ₹12 lakh to cover the risk of default on the payment of EMIs, etc.

The concept of pledging is similar, but the amount released by the broker after accepting your mutual funds, bonds or equity as collateral, can only be used for trading purposes. Since these funds remain in your trading account and cannot be withdrawn, there are no monthly obligations or payments like EMIs.

And the valuation processes are much simpler and straight forward. Every broker maintains a list of shares, mutual funds, bonds that they accept as collateral. We intend to keep GOI bonds as collateral and brokers typically provide 90% of their value to our trading account.

In the case of a traditional loan you have to pay interest on the full sanctioned amount of loan, even if you actually use only a part of it. Typically, banks also tend to discourage you to pre-pay the unused loan amount in order to enable you to reduce your interest burden.

In case of trading, however, the amount of money we utilize out of the sanctioned pledge amount is totally upon us. We may choose to utilize 10%, 50%, 100%, or not trade at all — there are no charges, penalties or hidden costs.

Pledging is what the smart rich do to make more money. I suggest you ought to research on how they use it to their advantage. One famous example is how Elon Musk used his Tesla shares as a pledge to raise funds to buy Twitter.

Elon did not use cash to buy Twitter. Let us just look at the possibilities he opened by doing so — the numbers are tweaked to explain the concept and are not a representation of the actual figures.

Let us assume Elon's shares in Tesla were worth ₹10,000 crore. These are just numbers in the computer and do not translate into any cash in his hand. If the Tesla share price goes up by 2% the next day, Elon's net worth will also go up by 2%, and so on

The only way to convert this into cash is to sell the shares to someone else in exchange for cash. But once you do that, you can't take advantage of any future price rise in Tesla stock.

So let us assume Elon has no cash with him but needs money to buy Twitter. Let us also say Twitter is worth ₹3,000 crore. Now, Elon has two ways to fund this purchase:

1. Either Elon must sell one-third of his shares in Tesla; or
2. Pledge just above one-third of his shares to a bank for a loan.

If he selects the first option, Elon will surely obtain ₹3,333 crore. But he will have a tax liability of 33%, which means he will have less than ₹2,200 crore left with him.

On the other hand if Elon pledges his shares to a bank, the bank will keep his Tesla share certificates and provide him a loan. In the worst case if Elon is unable to repay the debt, the bank will then sell his shares for cash in the open market.

Let us assume Elon does not default; instead, he repays the loan regularly. The biggest advantage he gets here is that he does not have to pay a single penny as tax. Also, the interest that he incurs on the loan from the bank is tax deductible as business expense.

This is just an example to encourage you to research on your own about this beautiful privilege that is out there.

We are going to do the same thing here, except of course the amounts are comparatively smaller — but the concept remains the same.

The ₹20 lakh of debt funds that you have bought can be pledged with the broker. By doing so, you are able to activate these funds for your trading activity. The broker enables only 90% of the value of these funds towards our trading account, the rest 10% is called a haircut.

What this means is that if you pledge ₹20 lakh worth of funds, the broker provides only ₹18 lakh as tradeable capital. The remaining ₹2 lakh forms the haircut.

This haircut is the broker's cushion for risk control and it is standard across almost all the top brokers. In the worst case if you wipe out your account — the broker can use this haircut value to offset its costs.

Keep in mind, the ₹20 lakh worth of debt funds are still in your name and the benefits from them, interest, etc. will flow only to you. It is like a lien marked against your holding in the name of the broker. If you wish to sell these stocks or debt funds in the future, you need to first unpledge them. These days unpledging is also instantaneous and a sell order can be placed the very next second.

The best part is you do not have to pay the broker any fees or interest for this feature. It is a system accepted by NSE and SEBI. The funds are still in your name and the broker cannot execute a sell or pledge or unpledge without your permission.

In the worst case even if your broker goes bankrupt, or intentionally commits fraud, your funds will still be safe as if these are held in demat form. Even after all these fail-safe policies if you still think you have been duped by the broker — there is a SCORES complaint system available *via* the SEBI grievance portal.

Brokers might charge you a flat fee during the pledging and un-pledging process. It is normally ₹30 per fund. So if you are pledging ₹20 lakh, you need to pay a flat fee of ₹30 as pledging request fee — not a big deal, you'll agree!

Let me walk you through the process on how to make your GOI bonds eligible for pledging. I am citing the process at Zerodha as the example. The process for other brokers might be somewhat different.

Step 1: You need to buy the GOI Bonds / G-Secs *via* open market. Let's assume you would have already done this.

Step 2: Visit your Portfolio >> Holdings page and click on the three dots showing against the scrip.

Step 3: Click on the "Pledge for margin" option.

Step 4: You will get an option to enter the QTY and then the applicable % haircut and the final "collateral margin available" will be displayed.

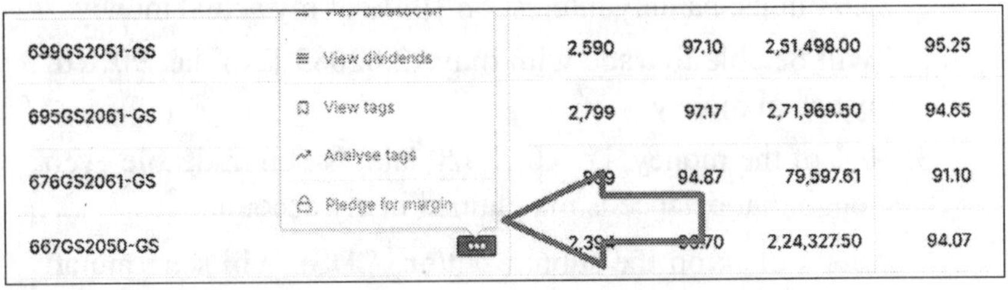

Figure 6.1: **Steps to Pledge GOI Bonds**

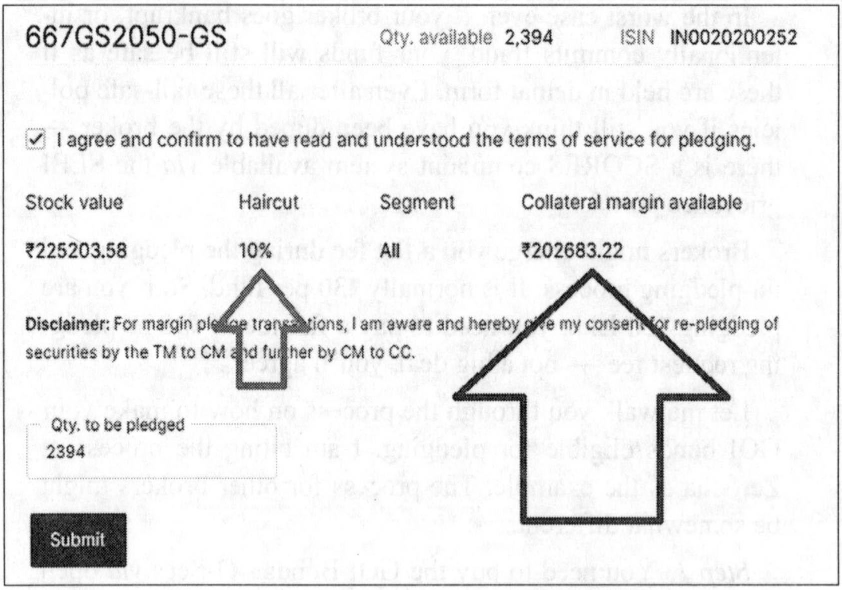

Figure 6.2: **Haircut and Collateral Split Up**

In the example selected I had a stock value of ₹2.25203 lakh and the final margin provided by the broker was ₹2.02683 lakh, i.e. 90% of my funds.

Some important points:

1. I will still be eligible to get the yearly interest for the entire 23,94 units, namely interest on 100% of my actual money.
2. I will be able to trade with only ₹2.02683 lakh, i.e. 90% of my actual money.
3. 10% of the money, i.e. ₹0.22520 lakh is non tradeable even though that balance is maintained in my account.

After I click on the submit button, CDSL will send me an email or SMS listing the steps to confirm and authorize the pledge. Once the OTP is entered and validated you will get the success message.

From the next day you will be able to use this fund for your trading activity.

At the time of this writing, you will be charged ₹30+GST for this process. This charge will be shown in the cash ledger.

Each broker has a similar process for pledging. Also, the depository services could be NSDL or CDSL depending on the broker you select.

Even before you buy a scrip, check with your broker about the steps required so that you have absolute clarity. We would never want to purchase a scrip only to learn that the broker will not accept it as a collateral-pledge!

The most important reason why I recommend that you pledge GOI bonds or G-Secs is mainly because this instrument has no downside risk. And you get a safe and secure interest income every year.

Pledging is available even for common stock or equity mutual funds. But these could have daily value fluctuations, i.e. stocks could make insane up or down moves which will impact the level of trading funds available.

The first thing we need to know is the funds that we have kept for capital are safe and sound. This is the foundation on which we can build other things.

In the above example, I am 100% confident that the fluctuation on the pledged value of ₹2.02683 lakh is not going to be very high. This will give you the confidence to take a trade that has say a margin requirement of up to 99% value of pledged holdings.

In case we wish to remove their pledged status, there is an option to "UNPLEDGE"; clicking on that will load another option where we can enter the QTY we wish to unpledge.

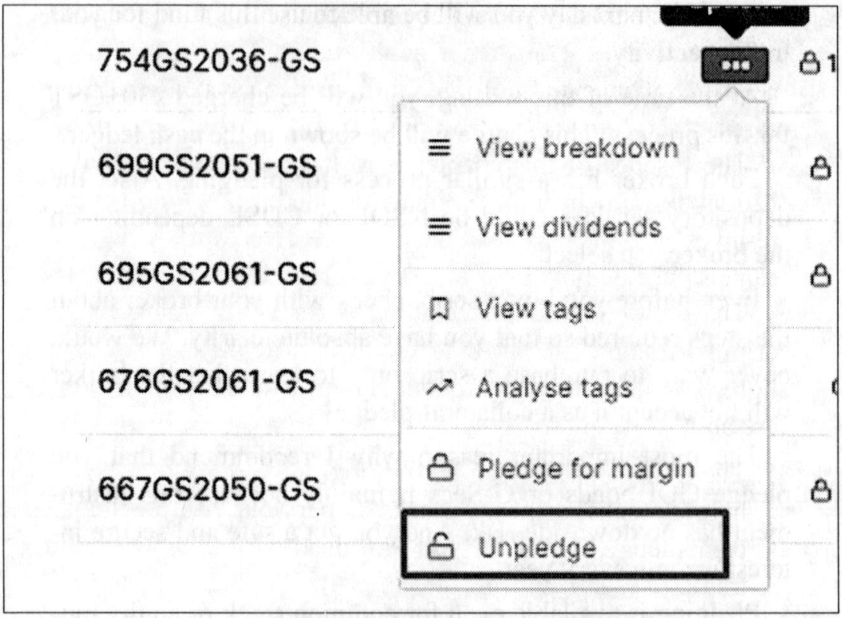

Figure 6.3: **Steps to Unpledge GOI Bonds**

Once the unpledged request is taken, within the next trading day these bonds will be visible in the holdings section and we could proceed to buy or sell them like common stock.

Figure 6.4: **Specify Quantity to Unpledge**

As I write this, Zerodha has introduced instant unpledge facility, wherein the customer can directly sell the bonds. We need not manually unpledge it; Zerodha's system will take care of that.

The essence of this chapter is to have a trading capital of ₹20 lakh in a debt fund. You can decide on how you want to re-invest the interest payments you receive every year. You can also decide how to re-invest your monthly trading profits.

The only commitment required is for you to maintain the original trading capital of ₹20 lakh in a debt fund. As highlighted earlier, this is the foundation on which the other floors are built.

1. The trading profits can be invested into equity, or debt, or hybrid stocks, or penny stocks as per your risk profile and competency. Even if you go dead-wrong, your future trading system will not get impacted as the foundation is still intact.
2. You should never get into a loss strategy that exceeds your emergency fund (more of that in Section 4), or else the foundation will be at stake.
3. Whatever you do, losing the original capital should not be a part of the plan. You may bet the profits you make for a new trade, but never the original capital of ₹20 lakh.

I strongly urge you to maintain strict self-discipline because trading options is like driving a car which is a hundred times more powerful than you are.

1. It can take you places.
2. Or, it can crash you to death.

What actually happens depends on how you drive it.

7

~

How to Select a Broker Based on Your Trading Style

THIS IS THE MOST DIFFICULT PART of being in the trading business. You need to be associated with a broker to punch your trading orders.

A broker is someone who will provide you the user interface, or the software or APIs (application programming interface, i.e. access to connect the broker's system from a third party application, mainly for algorithmic trading) to place, modify or cancel your trading orders. You will also be able to view the orders you've placed and executed.

Trading and investing are two completely different matters. Many people however do not sufficiently understand the difference between the two. Trading has an element of short term "time" in it, whereas the time factor is open-ended in investing. A trader has a specific plan about when to enter and exit a trade whereas an investor might be concerned only about when to enter to start with.

Ideally, trading should be treated as a profession and stock and mutual fund holdings as long-term investments. A profession could be challenging, boring, miserable or exciting from time-to-time. But investments should be like a solid rock — dependable and predictable.

Assets are something that continue to give you income even without your direct involvement. A house that is let out for rent is an asset — you do not have to visit your tenant every day; you will get the rent on time even if you visit them once a month.

A car takes you from one place to another, but it is not an asset unless you have tagged with Uber and receive a taxi-income from it.

The ₹20 lakh you invested into GOI bonds is an asset because it is going to give you income till the tenure of the bonds ends, requiring zero upkeep or maintenance.

The stocks that you invest in will be assets only if their value appreciates, or you receive good dividends from them. Meanwhile the stocks that nose-dive in value will become a burden for you. Only if a stock continues to appreciate does it become a worthwhile investment.

Trading, on the other hand, is very much like a job or a business. We are not really concerned whether the stock or index is going up or down, or moving within a range. We trade based on a strategy, and if the strategy is right — we gain. If the strategy is wrong — we end up losing.

Now the same broker can help you trade or invest, or both.

In order to trade you also need a trading account; whereas in order to invest you need a demat account. The futures and options trades are contracts most of which have an expiration value. Whereas any shares you buy can be held for a long time.

This preservation happens *via* a demat account. None of the trading entries go into demat, only the investments are held there. Basically the investments go to your "Holdings" or "Investments" section and the active traded instruments are logged in the "Positions" section.

~

These were the easy things that you just learned. There are a truck-load of learnings left about what you can do *via* the broker account. It might even take a month to learn the kind of regulatory reports the brokers send you.

We are not getting into the details as we need not know everything to get started.

Personally, I have experienced the trading / demat accounts with the following brokers — Zerodha, Kotak Securities, Paytm, 5Paisa, Finvasia, Mstock, ICICI Direct, Geojit, Alice Blue, HDFC Securities. The reason to try out so many brokers was due to specific features each of them offered.

Sometimes a particular broker did not offer a particular feature I wanted, so I had to find another broker who could offer it. My experience is that no broker has all the features in-built, and each broker has some pros and cons.

If you are a beginner and wish to start right, Zerodha would be the best choice for you. Their charts, ordering system and profit / loss reports are the easiest to understand.

In our case we are specifically interested in brokers who can provide pledging, margin collateral facility for GOI bonds, (G-Secs) we purchase.

So it is not a bad idea to contact each broker offline, or *via* their support portal and get your doubts clarified. Well, most of them also have zero account opening charges — so you do not lose money, but time.

Usually, brokerage and tax charges will be between 15% and 25% of the income for a seasoned trader. In other words, if s/he generates a monthly income of ₹1 lakh, almost ₹25,000 goes as brokerage + STT + stamp duty + other exchange charges.

If you are not profitable enough, the combination of brokerage and transaction charges could easily erode your hard-earned capital. Logically, stock market trading is a zero-sum game because every time you trade, the broker and government make money irrespective of whether you win or lose — you end up paying brokerage.

This puts additional pressure on a trader to perform big, and the only way out is to increase our earning potential. Saying so is easy, doing it is tough.

Over the last 15 years, brokerage charges have come down from 3% per value traded to a fixed ₹20 per lot. There are brokers who even provide free brokerage plans. It is not a bad idea to evaluate the 3 to 5 top brokers and then select one most in synch with your trading style.

A few other considerations you need to keep in mind are:

1. Quality of the broker's software;
2. Quality of their charting system;
3. Ability to punch orders quickly;
4. Easy to understand ledger, bills and account statements;
5. Transparent cash deposit / withdrawal system;
6. Ability of their customer care staff to address problems.

Of late many free brokerage providers ran into IT and server issues. If the ability to place, modify or delete the orders does not work — there is no significant advantage in going with a free broker.

Options trading has a higher risk element as we make use of leverage, so our ability to enter and exit any trade with lightning speed is very important. Sometimes a trading opportunity may last for only a few minutes. If your broker is too slow to punch the orders — you may not be able to grab such a trading opportunity.

The quality of the charting software is also equally important. We are going to base our trading on technical analysis, which requires charts and indicators. If the data feed that plots the chart is delayed or inaccurate then, too, we may miss out on a crucial opportunity. TradingView is an independent chart provider, their charts are intuitive, easy to use, and reliable. Luckily most new-generation brokers have a tie-up with TradingView and you will be able to get a ton of features free of cost.

These days practically all new generation brokers offer similar features. They all have an intuitive mobile app and the various features are easy to learn and use. Usually, you do not have to call up their customer care desk unless you run into a glitch or software issue.

Before you punch in big orders, you must know the steps to reach their helpline quickly. You might have to call up their "CALL and TRADE" desk during technical glitches or server issues to square off the positions.

Remember that you don't need to be married to a broker. You have the right and freedom to change your broker if things are not working out. The only disadvantage I see is the down-time it takes to transfer one's stock holdings, mutual funds from one broker to another.

Section

~

3

8

Basic Options Terminology

OPTIONS ARE FINANCIAL INSTRUMENTS whose value is derived from common stocks or indices, or any other tradeable asset.

Even if you have had no formal introduction to the financial markets, you would be familiar with what a stock is. A stock represents an ownership share in a company. You become a shareholder, i.e. a part owner, of the company whose stock you purchase.

For example, if company XYZ has listed a total of 1,00,000 shares, each of face value ₹100, then the total market value of XYZ would be ₹1 crore (100000 × 100). And if you hold one share of this firm, you are a 0.001% owner.

Derivatives which track the price, time and volatility of the XYZ company's share price are called option contracts.

Now if XYZ is an important firm and if we group the topmost companies to represent the sector or economy — then that's called an index.

This book's scope is limited only to index options. We are limiting our focus and scope in order to increase our chances of survival and success. While there are more than 4,000 listed companies in India, the number of tradeable indices are currently only four to six.

In contrast to an individual share, an index has a lower risk of large price movement arising from insider trading, frauds, price-fixing, manipulation, etc. Individual stocks could be manipulated but it is far more difficult to manipulate the price movements of an index. In order to manipulate an index, the fraudster would have to simultaneously buy / sell 5 to 8 stocks at the same time. This is usually not possible for individuals or small firms as they would be handling only limited funds.

So we are planning to trade index options to insulate ourselves from any manipulations and fraud. The level of certainty an index provides is much greater than a component stock.

Let's look at the example in Figure 8.1. I have compared ADANIENT *versus* Nifty50 on the daily time frame. Just look at the highlighted portion when the ADANIENT price started falling quite brutally.

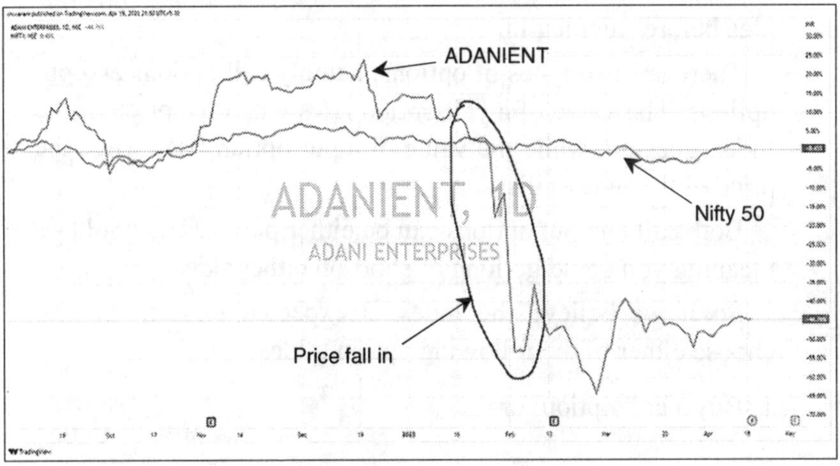

Figure 8.1: **Sharp Fall in a Stock Price *versus* Flat Line for the Index**

Meanwhile the Nifty50 index did not have a major fall. In fact, it held its ground. ADANIENT is a component of the Nifty50 index. What this shows is trading on indices will give a higher probability of safety and sanity.

The main indices for which you can trade futures and options in NSE and BSE are:

1. Nifty50 — An index comprising the top 50 companies of India, and serves as the benchmark.
2. BankNifty — An index comprising the stocks of India's top banks.
3. Sensex — tracks 30 top companies in India. The oldest index, also now appears for F&O trading.

We will consider the Nifty50 index for the strategies, payoff calculations and examples in this book.

The best place to start learning options will be the Zerodha varsity authored by Karthik Rangappa.*

I will cover a few of the basics here so that you have a fair idea before stepping in.

There are two types of options, namely call options and put options. The value of a call option rises when the price of the Index goes up, while the value of a put option rises when the price of the Index falls.

Both call and put options can be either purchased or sold — meaning you could go long or short on either side.

So if we believe the Index is expected to rise, we can choose either of the following option trades:

1. Buy a call option; or

---

* *Options Theory for Professional Trading* — Varsity by Zerodha: Options is a contract where the price of the options is based on an underlying. The contract grants the buyer the right… zerodha.com

2. Sell a put option.

Alternately, if we expect the Index to fall, then the following two option trades are possible.

1. Buy a put option; or
2. Sell a call option.

These are just the basics. In the real world there are several combinations possible to favorably handle the movement of an index.

Essentially, there are only three major market movements possible that we need to be aware of:

1. Strong upward movement (uptrend / bullish market).
2. Strong downward movement (down trend / bearish market).
3. Range based movement (non-directional market).

Even though there are only three possible theoretical market moves, namely up, down and flat — the number of strategies that can be deployed by combining option strikes is infinite.

If you have a bullish view, a single-legged strategy would be as simple as buying a call option.

A two-legged strategy could be a debit spread, namely buying a call option, and selling a higher put option.

An example of three-legged strategy could be a "Bull Call Ladder", etc. Similarly, there are 5-, 6- and 7-legged strategies as well. You can use any free option strategy builder to design, test and deploy such strategies.

The Black-Scholes-Merton option pricing model highlights the following factors that affect the price (premium) of option strikes:

1. Change in price of the underlying asset (**delta**).
2. The amount of time remaining till expiration of the option contract (**theta**).
3. The volatility of the underlying asset (**vega**).

4. Change in the risk-free interest rate (**rho**).
5. Dividends declared by the stock; but since we are considering only index options, we can ignore this.

Delta measures how much an option's price will change with respect to a change in the underlying asset's price. If the delta of a particular option strike is, say, 50%, it means that if the price of the underlying moves by 100 points, the option's price will change by 50%, i.e. it would move by 50 points. Similarly, if a strike has a delta of 13%, it would mean that the option's price would change by 13 points for every 100-point change in the price of the underlying. Option strikes are predefined intervals on which option contracts of puts and calls are created.

The option strikes are represented in a tabular format, with the Call strikes mentioned toward the left and the Put strikes to the right. This tabular representation is called an option chain. Usually, the center portion, which denotes the current level at which Nifty50 is trading is called "At the Money" (ATM). The Call option strikes with a lower value than the current trading price will be called "In the Money" (ITM), this is true for all the Put option strikes with a higher value than the current value. Similarly, the Call option strikes higher and the Put option strikes lower than the current trading price are called "Out of the Money" OTM

For illustration, if we consider the current trading price of Nifty50 as 23420, then the ATM strike will be 23400. ITM option strikes will always be highlighted / greyed so the user can easily identify them from the option chain. The ITM strikes of the Call options are 23350, 23300, 23250, and all values lower than 23400. The ITM strikes of the Put options are 23450, 23500, 23550 and all values above 23400.

					CALLS			PUTS						
Gamma	Vega	Theta	Delta	OI-lakh	Call OI	LTP	Strike ↓	LTP	Put OI	OI-lakh	Delta	Theta	Vega	Gamma
0.0007	6	-14	0.83	1.4		355.40	23100	33.25		24.0	-0.17	-14	6	0.0007
0.0008	6	-16	0.79	0.7		315.00	23150	42.15		10.6	-0.21	-16	6	0.0008
0.0009	7	-17	0.75	3.8		275.00	23200	52.40		32.4	-0.25	-17	7	0.0009
0.001	8	-19	0.70	2.0		237.50	23250	65.55		12.1	-0.30	-19	8	0.001
0.0011	8	-20	0.65	11.3		204.15	23300	80.45		40.0	-0.35	-20	8	0.0011
0.0012	8	-20	0.59	10.7		171.50	23350	98.45		21.9	-0.41	-20	8	0.0012
0.0012	9	-21	0.53	41.4		142.90	[illegible]	119.45		48.4	-0.47	-21	9	0.0012
0.0012	9	-20	0.47	21.7		116.30	23450	143.70		18.7	-0.53	-20	9	0.0012
0.0012	8	-20	0.41	73.7		93.75	23500	170.45		43.6	-0.59	-20	8	0.0012
0.0012	8	-19	0.35	31.6		73.85	23550	201.10		17.5	-0.65	-19	8	0.0012
0.0011	7	-17	0.29	60.5		57.00	23600	233.70		20.1	-0.71	-17	7	0.0011
0.001	7	-15	0.24	17.7		43.10	23650	271.00		5.5	-0.76	-15	7	0.001
0.0009	6	-13	0.19	45.5		32.40	23700	310.00		10.0	-0.81	-13	6	0.0009

Figure 8.2: **Option Chain Depicting the Various Calls and Puts and their Premiums for 27 April 2023**

Similarly, the OTM strikes of the Call options are 23450, 23500, 23550, and all values higher than 23400. The OTM strikes of the Put options are 23350, 23300, 23250, and all values lower than 23400. OTM strikes are represented in plain white background free from any highlights or grey markings.

The strike interval for Nifty50 is 50 points, i.e. 23400, 23450, 23500 etc. If Nifty goes up by 50 points, the new ATM will become 23450, and the ITM highlights will change immediately. The new Call ITMs will be 23400, 23350 and lower and the new Put ITMS will be 23500, 23550 and above. Similarly, the OTM strikes will also be revised by 50 points, the new Call OTMs will be 23500, 23550 and above and the new Put OTMs will be 23400, 23350 and below.

You might have also noticed that each of the strike intervals has a Last Traded Price (LTP) for both the Call option as well as the Put option. When Nifty50 increases in value, all the Call options appreciate and the Put options depreciate in value. Similarly, if Nifty50 drops, then the Call options depreciate and the Put options appreciate in value.

I trust you now have a basic idea on what options are. Let us now discuss how the Theta and Vega greeks affect option prices.

Let us consider an example. Say, Nifty closes exactly at 23400 on 21 November 2024. In that case, 23400 CE and PE will both go to zero. Currently 23400 CE has a value of ₹142.9 and 23400 PE has a value of ₹119.45.

To know the value of the contract, the premium of the strike will have to be multiplied by its lot multiplier. Nifty's lot multiplier is set as 25 at the time of working this book.* The exchanges could change this lot multiplier anytime, it

* The lot multiplier is decided by the exchange and they could revise the count based on few parameters.

may go to 50, 75 or 100 depending on the market conditions and the regulatory framework set by the SEBI.

To know how much money to pay to buy an option contract, you need to multiply the premium with its lot size.

So in rupee terms if both go to zero then the value left in them would be: 142.9 × 25 + 119.45× 25 = ₹6558.75.

We have less than one week, i.e. 3 more trading days left till the expiry on 21 November. The value of these options is mostly theta (time value). Suppose on Tuesday, too, Nifty50 closed at 23400,then the same 23400 CE and PE would have depreciated by approximately 25% to 30%. And if prices remain the same on Wednesday as well, the option premiums will drop approximately another 25% to 30% .

Theta is the Greek variable that tracks the time left in the contract.

The rule is that all ATM (At the Money) and OTM (Out of the money) option premiums will become zero at the end of the expiry day. So whatever value it holds currently is because of the "time factor", namely "Theta".

The only strikes that would have intrinsic value are ITMs. If Nifty expires at 23400, then 23350 CE would be ITM1, 23300 would be ITM2 etc. The final premiums would be ₹50 for 23350 and ₹100 for 23300, namely the same as the strike interval.

Options were originally invented as a hedging tool to protect investors. For example, suppose you have adequate stakes in India's top 5 stocks, namely HDFC Bank, RELIANCE, INFY, ICICI Bank, and ITC. And you are apprehensive that there could be a price decline in each of these apprehensive stocks due to some news/event like, say, an upcoming RBI monetary policy announcement.

Yet you do not wish to sell the shares for this event. For downside protection you choose to buy a Put option on Nifty50, so that even if its price goes down your Put option will reward you and make up for any loss due to a fall in the prices of your bank stocks.

Now the person who took the position opposite to yours, i.e. who sold the put option to you, would have done so speculating that Nifty50 will not fall.

Now, suppose after the event Nifty50 in fact does not go down, you will lose the premium you paid, whereas your counterpart speculator gains the premium.

So, both of you are happy:

1. You are happy because the shares you held did not decline in value, and you were okay to pay some insurance for protection against any possible downside.
2. The speculator is happy because his view turned out to be correct he made money off you.

We are trying to be that speculator here. We neither plan to hold on to stock positions nor use options as a hedging tool to protect our portfolio. We will be using options purely as a trading tool. We have a market view and then plan option trading strategies based on our view.

Volatility represented by the Greek symbol **Vega** is also a major factor that decides an option's premium. Of the three greeks, namely Delta, Theta, and Vega, Vega is the most complicated to explain. At any specific instant we can calculate the Delta by checking the last traded price. Similarly, we can calculate Theta by measuring the time remaining in the contract. But Vega measures the uncertainty of price change. This uncertainty is called volatility and it is the major reason we have price fluctuations every day.

On any traded day, a stock or index experiences price swings due to the ongoing auction process between the buyers and sellers. If buyers expect the stock's price to go up soon, they will be ready to buy it now. Correspondingly, if sellers expect the stock's price could fall in future, they will be ready to sell the same now.

A change in fundamentals, such as quarterly results, news, or events could significantly influence such price swings, thereby pumping up the volatility.

Higher the volatility, higher will be the option's premium (price). Higher the uncertainty — higher will be the volatility. Going back to the same example, if there is an emergency meeting scheduled by the RBI Governor — the same 23400 CE and PE could suddenly surge in prices.

So even though the price of the underlying remains the same, an increase in volatility will trigger a surge in option premium.

Before you start trading in the futures and options segment, you should try and understand the Options Pricing Model and Black-Scholes-Merton theory in detail. Typically, most traders look only at Delta and tend to totally ignore the Theta and Vega greeks. I suggest you should give each of the three variables their due weightage. By doing so, your trading results will improve.

The fourth variable that influences option prices is the interest rate set by RBI. Normally, interest rates do not change every day or every week and there are scheduled days when RBI announces its interest rate decision. On a practical case-to-case basis, therefore, interest rates can normally be ignored for the purpose of predicting option prices.

So we have now covered three important aspects that determine an option's price:

1. Market direction.
2. The time left till expiration.
3. Volatility of the underlying stock or index, etc.

Now you would have heard the saying, "The trend is your friend." What this means is that you can make money if you know the likely future direction of the market.

In options trading, though, you can make money even if you are not sure about the trend ahead. Time and volatility are the other two variables using which we can earn profits even if we get the first one wrong. Usually in stock trading and futures, you need to buy first and then sell at a higher price to generate profits, i.e. you can make money only in one direction. Whereas in options trading you can make money in all three directions, namely up, down or sideways.

This is the main reason why trading options is much more powerful than trading stocks. To do that we need to educate ourselves about the effects of time and volatility. "Time should be your dearest friend and volatility should not be your enemy," should be the new saying in the world of options trading!

~

9

Simple Options Trading Strategies

LET US NOW CONSIDER a few practical situations and understand how options trading provides great solutions for them all.

To make money in stock markets you need to buy shares at a low price and sell at higher prices.

Let's say that company XYZ is trading at ₹95. Based on your research, you conclude that it is a good buy. And then wait for its price to go above ₹110 to sell it and pocket the profit of ₹15 per share.

Honestly, do you know any methods of making money in stock markets other than this?

That's where options trading comes in handy. With options you can make money even if the stock price itself is not moving. Thus, if the stock price of firm XYZ was trading at ₹95 on 2 November 2024 and the price remained the same ₹95 on 28 November 2024 — you can still make money using options.

Did I get your attention? If yes, let us look at the examples that follow.

Let's assume Nifty index was at 23400 on 28 November 2024.

View-1: Nifty will rise to 24400 by 26 December, i.e. there would be an up move of 1,000 points in one month. This is a purely bullish view and either buying a 23400 CE or selling a 23400 PE will make you money if the up move occurs.

View-2: Nifty will be at 22400 by 26 December, i.e. it will fall by 1,000 points in one month. If you have such a clear bearish view, either buying a 23400 PE or selling a 23400 CE will make you money.

View-3: Nifty will end between 23100 to 23700 by 26 December. To profit from this range-bound view, you would need a combination of options. Short iron condor or short iron fly option strategies could help you make money if this view plays out.

View-4: Nifty will be at 23500 by 26 December 2024. This is only a moderately bullish view. So we might need a combination of strategies, such as a long call spread or a short put spread to profit from this view. Thus, for example, you could buy 23400 CE, and sell 23500 CE (a debit spread), or sell 23500 PE, and buy 23400 PE (a credit spread).

View-5: Nifty will be 23300 by 26 December 2024. This is a moderately bearish view. The appropriate option trading strategy to profit from such a view could be either a long put spread or a short call spread; you could buy 23400 PE, and sell 23300 PE (a debit spread), or sell 23300 CE, and buy 23400 CE (credit spread).

These are the only 5 basic possibilities you need to contend with now. Just think about it — where would Nifty be on 26 Dec and just cross check if any of the above 5 views are unable to fulfil it.

This book's scope is limited to just three option trading strategies. That's because that's all we really need to deploy whatever be one's market view.

1. Short iron fly;
2. Credit spreads; and
3. Debit spreads.

These three strategies can be deployed with the capital that we have pledged. So we need not bring in additional funds for trading. And, believe me, if we narrow down the scope of learning to a niche area — we can become an expert faster.

Options trading is the most difficult segment of the stock market to make money in. That's because there is a limited time factor involved. Think about this: you buy 1 share of XYZ @ ₹95 on 28 November and there is a time limit till 26 December. The available choices for you then are either to sell at profit, or lose the entire ₹95. How would that make you feel?

Just because there are no time restrictions by the exchanges or the markets, people keep buying stocks and holding them for a lifetime. If there were a time limit they would probably have exited, whether profitably or at a loss.

As we have seen, this time factor (called Theta) is one of the important variables that influences option premiums because all options come with an expiry date. There are options expiring every week, every month, and every year.

The beauty of Index options is that these have weekly expiries whereas stock options expire once a month. Let us take the example of Nifty50, where options expire every Thursday. This also means that we get to plan and deploy one Nifty50 options strategy every week, or four strategies a month.

The advantage of trading with a weekly target is that you get hands-on experience quickly and the learning curve is faster. Just like any other profession, you only get better when you practice.

Once you have grasped the basics on how option expiry works, you can move on to monthly or yearly / LEAPS (options above one year). The longer the expiry date, the higher will be the premiums, and slower will be the time decay.

If, however, you have a regular job and wish to learn options trading during your spare time — focusing on monthly expiries is a better idea. That way you need to deploy only a single strategy each month. You will then have ample time and mind space to adjust your positions, firefight, or book profit / loss.

Many people mistakenly consider stock markets to be a lottery system where you enter with a small stake and take home a truck-load of winnings. That rarely happens. And even if it did — the person will subsequently be forced to give it back to the market, and end up being poorer and miserable.

Money will not flow to you unless you have acquired adequate financial knowledge and expertise. Only years of experience, exposure and discipline will teach you that. Winning ₹1 out of ₹100 spent works out to be a 1% daily return.

You will have an annual percentage profit of 3,678% if you just earn just 1% a day.

Well, that may not be practical. Let us start with just a 1% return every month if that's okay with you!

~

10

~

Advanced Options Trading Strategies with Fixed Losses

IN THE PREVIOUS CHAPTER WE DISCUSSED the factors that influence option prices. We are going to analyze each one of them in depth with examples so that you get the required know-how.

Directional Strategies

The easiest way to make money would be the ability to reasonably forecast the future trend, i.e. to be able to figure out whether the price is going to rise or fall. If your assessment turns out to be correct then it is easy to deploy a directional option strategy to take advantage of this.

It is, however, tough to accurately predict the market's future direction — even the best technical analysts can achieve only 70% accuracy, if that.

How to get the direction right? It is a tough job, and you need hours and hours of experience of watching price action, marking the appropriate levels on a chart, and testing your skills.

Let no one deceive you: stock market is not a place where you can make easy money. It is a place where you will be rewarded proportionally to the efforts and skills you apply.

A good start would be to take a course on technical analysis. Zerodha Varsity has a free starter course on this, but for options trading you might require advanced knowledge and that would take hours of study over and above the free starter course.

When I started on technical analysis, I would use 6 or 7 indicators on my chart and it began to look complex. Bollinger bands, MACD, RSI, ATR, SuperTrend, ADX + DMI, three types of EMA were all on the same chart. Once I started gaining confidence, I removed five of the indicators. Currently, I only use the ADX+DMI and EMAs on my chart and it looks far more elegant and actionable.

Even after observing each and every 5-minute candle of Nifty50 for a period of three years, without skipping even a single day, my accuracy for directional guess is just barely above 50% — and I've learnt to live with that!

Handling the other 50% when you are wrong is the biggest challenge. When you deploy a directional options strategy — the best way is *via* credit or debit spreads wherein the stop loss is, in effect, automatically loaded in your trade.

It's true that the reward is higher when you buy or sell naked options, but in doing so you are playing with fire. There is a high possibility that markets could prove your forecast wrong and wipe you out.

Also, it's impossible to put a stop loss for an overnight position. Even if it's an intraday situation, the stop loss is more of an art than science — and it would take you many, many more hours of learning and practice to perfect it.

As we go along, we will see examples of debit spreads and credit spreads, and weigh the pros and cons of each so that you get a basic idea about when to deploy each.

For the payoff chart and pictures I will be using an online software called Opstra (please note that I have no business affiliation with them and I am using their tool because it's free).

~

Nifty was at 23462 on 18 November 2024, and the current expiry was on Thursday, 21 November 2024.

Now, suppose you have a bullish view and expect Nifty to close above 23600 on the 21st. You can handle this trade by following either of the two strategies described below.

Figure 10.1: **Nifty 1-Hour Chart**

Strategy-1: Put Credit Spread

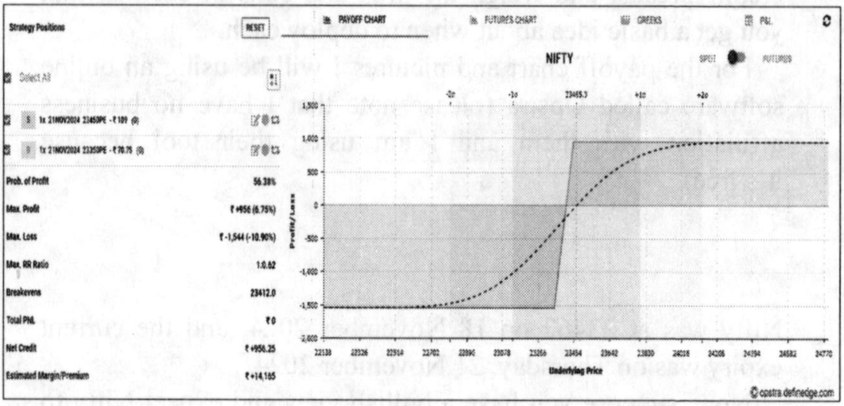

Figure 10.2: **Risk Payoff Diagram for Our Put Credit Spread**

Sell 23450 PE and Buy 23350 PE for hedge (*see* Figure 10.2).

23450 PE was trading at ₹109 and 23350 PE was trading at ₹70.75.

The maximum you could have gained from this trade was ₹956 [(₹109 – ₹70.75) × 25]. This will happen if Nifty were to close above 23450.

And if your market view is wrong, the maximum money you would lose is ₹1544 [(₹100 × 25) – 956].

Strategy-2: Call Debit Spread

Buy 23450 CE and sell 23550 CE for hedge (*see* Figure 10.3).

In this example, 23450 CE is trading at ₹121.45 and 23550 CE is available at ₹74.1.

The maximum you can gain from this trade is: 100 × 25 minus (121.45 – 74.1) × 25 = ₹1316. You will get this amount if Nifty closes at or above 23550.

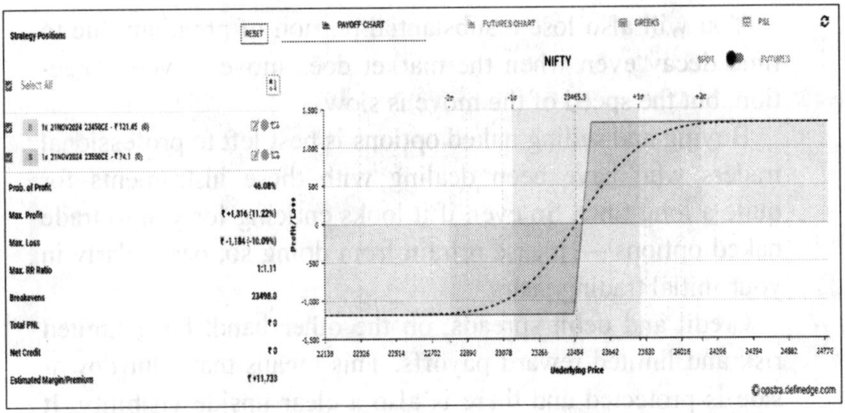

Figure 10.3: **Risk Payoff Diagram for Call Debit Spread**

And the maximum you can lose is (121.45 – 74.1) × 25 = ₹1183.75, if your view turns out to be wrong.

Now, since both strategies will make you money if your view turns out to be correct, how do you decide which strategy to deploy? The answer to that question will only come from experience and experimenting *via* trial and error.

Buying Naked Calls or Naked Puts Not Recommended

There is a specific reason that I did not list either buying a call (CE) or buying a put (PE) as a directional strategy even though those are the easiest methods available.

The reason is that buying a naked CE or a naked PE must be fully funded by cash in your ledger; you will not be able to use a margin pledge for such buying.

The other important reason is the high downside risk if your analysis turns out to be wrong. Both CE and PE will become worthless, i.e. you will lose the entire premium you pay, if markets do not move decisively in your direction.

You will also lose a substantial portion of premium due to time decay even when the market does move in your direction, but the speed of the move is slow.

Buying and selling naked options is best left to professional traders who have been dealing with these instruments for quite a long time. So even if it looks enticing for you to trade naked options — please refrain from doing so, particularly in your initial trading years.

Credit and debit spreads, on the other hand, have limited risk and limited reward payoffs. This means that your downside is protected and there is also a clear upside visibility. It might take much longer to build wealth *via* this route — but in the meantime it will help you learn technical analysis, price forecasting and how options contracts work.

Making money is one part. Equally important is getting your market view right. And, believe me, it's not that easy to do so. You need to work hard to improve your market analysis.

Let us review the worst case for the two strategies described above. If you deploy Strategy-1, your maximum loss is ₹1,544 whereas in the case of Strategy-2 the maximum expected loss was ₹1,184. Neither of these losses will burn a hole in your pocket. You also have a fail-safe, i.e. guaranteed income *via* interest payments from GOI bonds, this could fund your learning curve till you perfect your research.

If you visit YouTube and search "Make money in stock markets" you can see countless videos claiming "Guaranteed ways to make quick money," "100% working system", "Double your money in 1 month", etc. Let me reassure to you there is absolutely no guaranteed way to make money in stock markets.

"Anybody can become successful in stock markets," is a blatant lie. Only the best of the best can make money in stock markets. If you have the hunger to become the best, be among the top 5% — then it could work for you.

The research, analyze and test (RAT) cycle is what you need to become successful. Only then your views will be backed by solid rationale and you will have the conviction to deploy the correct strategies.

Both these strategies require you to provide a margin to the broker/exchange. Usually the broker will inform you the exact margin that is required to deploy this strategy. In the example quoted above the maximum margin works out to be approximately ₹14,165.

Since we have already pledged our GOI bonds we need not fund this ₹ 14,165 from our cash balance. It will get utilized from that pledge. And once we exit this position either by squaring off the trade or by letting it expire — then the blocked margin will get reversed (credited) to you.

Once this position was squared off on 21 November 2024 (expiry day), the entire amount got reversed (credited) to the ledger.

The broker will not charge you any amount, interest or fees for using your own margin money — it is absolutely free.

Now, the differences between credit and debit strategies are:

- The credit strategy will instantly credit ₹956, to your ledger, whereas
- With the debit strategy you need to have an extra cash balance of ₹1,316 in your account.

Directional strategies also always come with added psychological stress and frustration when markets go against your plan. If we have a bullish view but the market goes bearish — our position will go into loss. And, so, there is every reason for us to feel disappointed, dejected and a loser.

One of the reasons why people with high intelligence fail to become professional traders is because they are not ready to accept losses. From childhood we were all taught not to make mistakes.

Remember when you were a kid and you made a mistake, people around would scold, tease or punish you. If you failed an exam, the teacher would punish you. If you fell from a bicycle, people around you will make fun of you. You might still remember how bad people made you feel each time you failed.

In brief, we were taught that failing is a bad thing. Well, this may work best during school days — the fear of failure will help us prepare well for examinations. Peer pressure will force us to perform well in co-curricular activities and sports. Most of us may have earned a degree or got a job due to this fear of failure.

But in real life we need to respect and provide due weightage to failures. Failure need not be avoided, instead we need to analyze why we failed and improve from there.

Similarly, in trading failure is an important aspect. Only when we fail will we really know why our research went wrong. Only when we lose money, will we do a serious post-mortem.

Even the smartest trader fails 4 out of 10 times — how you keep your mind calm during those failures is what makes you a true champion.

Having a directional bias does not mean guess work. You should be able to forecast the market direction by scanning and analyzing charts. If you plan to just guess the direction without any research and deploy a strategy — even as failure will not teach you anything.

Since trading is an individual activity, we cannot find solace from co-workers, friends or peers. This means that we need to have a better mental capacity to handle failures and fears.

Non-Directional Strategies

Contrary to popular belief, markets stay range bound 90% of the time. While a breakout or a breakdown will catch public, news and media attention, no one really talks about range bound markets. That's because it is boring.

Countless books have been written on "trading breakouts," "chasing momentum," "chart patterns to trade breakouts", etc. Only 10% of the time do markets do that. Of course, that 10% of time is very exciting to see, watch and participate.

It is like a 50-over cricket match and our scoring rate has been at 5 runs per over till the 45-over stage. Then in comes MS Dhoni and hits three boundaries in the 46th over. Suddenly, people start talking and their friends too switch on the live-stream to watch the match.

In the last 5 overs the net run rate was 12 per over. Let us work out the math.

First 45 overs runs = 225, last 5 over runs = 60. Final score = 285. Approximately 80% of the total runs were made in the first 45 overs, but what do you think people will talk about? The last five overs, right? That's breakout trading for you.

Our focus here, however, is going to be on the earlier 45 overs, the boring part of the match but which contributed to 80% of the score.

Coming back to the markets, benchmark indices also have a natural tendency to grind slowly; staying mostly range bound as the bull and bears constantly wrestle . These are great times to deploy the non-directional strategies from our arsenal.

Markets break out or break down typically when the fundamentals change, such as on the basis of some important news, quarterly results or big-events. Marely expected good news is not enough; what is needed is big, breaking news. Examples could be:

1. RBI hikes repo rates by 75 basis points.
2. India's GDP grew by 7% *versus* 5% YoY.
3. ICICI Bank QoQ surges 60%, highest NII recorded.
4. Terrorists attack a Mumbai hotel.
5. China military clashes with Indian soldiers at LAC.
6. The ruling party loses a Lok sabha re-election.

These news events can occur during market hours, in which case we can handle the impact better. But such a news event occurring after market hours typically leads to a gap-up or gap-down opening the next day.

Gap-up or gap-down openings are very difficult to predict or handle and suddenly our profitable strategy may start accumulating losses. That's why it is very important not to carry your positions overnight — unless you know what you are doing.

All limited loss strategies could also be carried overnight — because we have 100% visibility on how much we could lose. Unlimited option strategies such as naked option selling have the leverage to wipe out your account — so it is better to stay away from those in your initial trading career.

Agreed the amount of income you generate will be lower using limited-loss strategies — but it would still be worth it.

Short Iron Fly

In this strategy, we sell ATM calls and puts and then buy OTM calls and puts for hedge.

For example: sell 23450 CE and PE and then buy 23650 CE and 23250 PE (Figure 10.5).

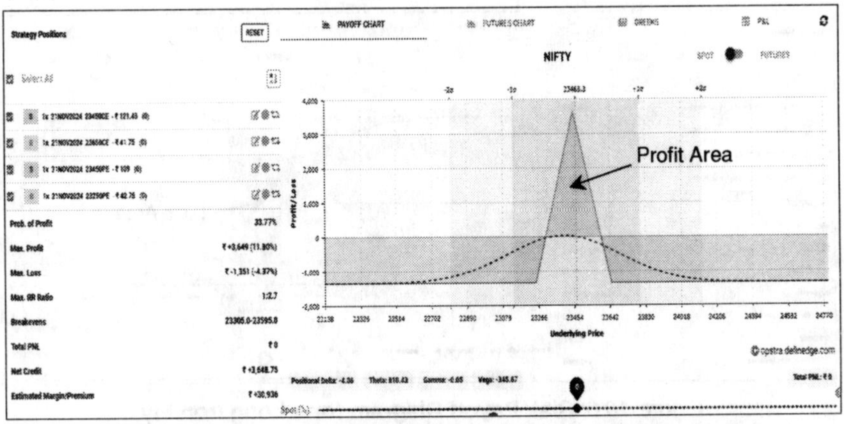

Figure 10.5: **Risk Payoff Diagram for Our Short Iron Fly Trade**

The maximum profit in this case will be ₹3,649 and the maximum loss will be ₹1,351. If Nifty manages to close in the range denoted in the grey color we will be profitable, i.e. between the Nifty levels of 23305 to 23595 in this particular case.

This strategy will require a margin of ₹30,936 which will automatically get blocked from the GOI bond pledge you have provided.

It is a net credit strategy, namely your ledger will be credited with ₹3,649 the moment you initiate this trade.

Long Iron Fly

Long iron fly is the opposite of the short iron fly and is used if we expect the markets to breakout or breakdown from a range. The important point to note is that with a long iron fly we need a huge movement to generate profits. Thus, this strategy is best suited if there are big macro events, such as an election, announcement of quarterly results, annual budget, inflation data, etc.

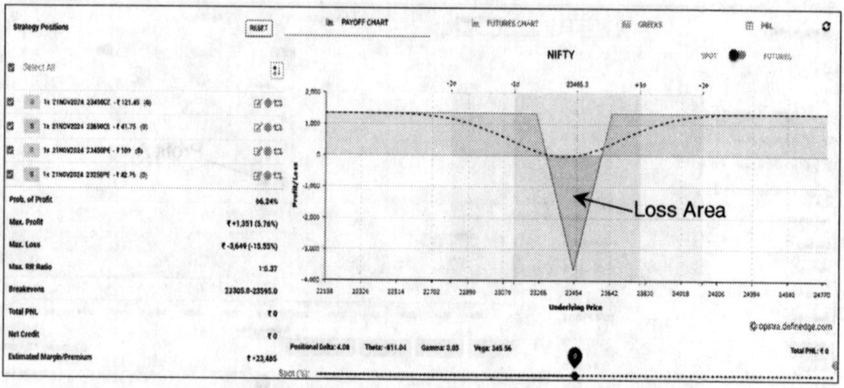

Figure 10.6: **Risk Payoff Diagram for a Long Iron Fly**

One thing is certain — both short iron fly and long iron fly will not make the money at the same time. Since one is the inverse of the other, only one of them will end in profits. The decision to choose the profitable one entirely depends on the trader and his research.

As can be seen in the Figure 10.6 we will make money only if Nifty either breaks down below the 23305 level, or breaks out above the 23595 level.

Short Iron Condor

Short iron condor is a variation of the short iron fly. Instead of shorting the ATM (at the money) strikes, we short-sell OTM2 or OTM3 out of the money strikes. Doing so alters the risk-payoff curve, making it look more like a plateau and not like a hill as we saw with the short iron fly.

There are three specific differences between the short iron fly and short iron condor:

1. The exact profit amount is more predictable for an iron condor *vis-a-vis* the iron fly.

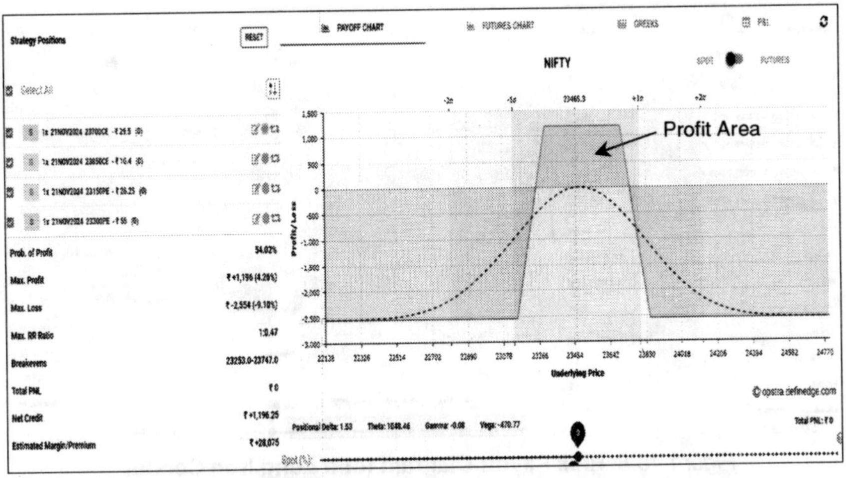

Figure 10.7: **Risk Payoff Diagram for a Short Iron Condor**

2. The breakeven range is much wider for an iron condor *vis-a-vis* the iron fly.
3. However, the risk-reward for the iron fly is much better than for an iron condor.

As an example:

- Call side: Sell 23700 CE and Buy 23850 CE;
- Put side: Sell 23300 PE and Buy 23150 PE.

As you would note, the maximum profit will be ₹1,196; and the maximum loss will be ₹2,554 both pre-determined. The breakeven range is wider and would lie between 23253 and 23747.

This strategy will require a margin of ₹28,075.

Long Iron Condor

The opposite of short iron condor, the long condor is a breakout / breakdown strategy. Here we expect the index to move by a large value to generate profits.

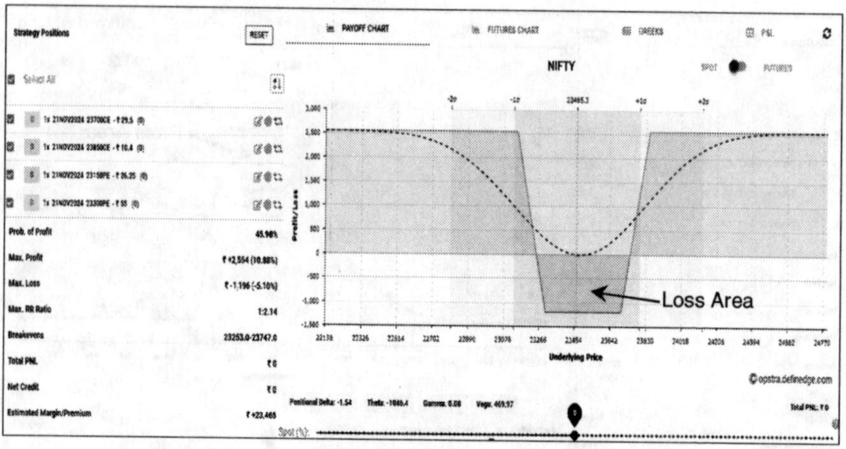

Figure 10.8: **Risk Payoff Diagram for a Long Iron Condor**

Breakout / breakdown trading works best during a macro event or a change in fundamentals. Here again, only one among the short iron condor or the long iron condor will be profitable at a time. Since the long iron condor is an inverse strategy of the short iron condor, the trader has to choose the right one based on his experience and research.

The long iron condor will make us money only if Nifty steps outside the range of 23253 to 23747 on other side.

A directional strategy would require you to research where Nifty might go by the 21st of November. A non-directional strategy, on the other hand, requires you to figure out where Nifty should not go!

This is the biggest advantage of trading options compared with normal stock trading. By trading options we can make money in all the three market scenarios:

- The market goes up;
- The market goes down;
- The market remains sideways.

It is again important to stress the point that while option strategies are easy to plan on paper, but you will run into losses if your research or home-work is not adequate. While these losses may not hurt you badly, but they will adversely affect your confidence.

There is absolutely no substitute to predicting the closing expiry for every trade. It's highly recommended that you do your own research instead of trusting the research of others, or news or tips. I agree that one's own research will take time to generate results — but that effort will payoff much better than you have expected.

It's important to also remember that non-directional strategies need not work all the time. If we select a weekly expiry, for example, we then have five trading days to reckon with. Markets may remain absolutely flat for four days, and then swing wildly on the fifth day spoiling our profits.

You must never get emotionally attached to the markets because the markets don't even know who you are. The direction the market trends, or reverses, is entirely up to it and we do not have any control over that. Feeling disheartened when your strategies run into losses needs to be handled. Only if we invest quality time and effort to understand price action, can we expect a higher accuracy from our research.

With experience you will also learn to book profits early. We may not get the full 100% juice when we prematurely close a profitable trade position — but remember we still did make profits. Hours of scanning charts will give you the edge necessary to assess whether the market is making a move against your position.

Fire Fighting Strategies

Consider this: as per your research you believe that it is going to be a directional market in the week ahead. But what if your assessment is wrong? How, then, can you limit your losses?

This is where fire-fighting strategies come in handy. They can work equally well with directional and non-directional strategies.

The basic idea is to enter a contrary position once your original position is in deep loss. This contra position's main objective will be to cut losses — but if planned wrongly, it could bleed you further.

Fire Fighting in a Directional Strategy

Suppose you had concluded that Nifty is going up and you get into a credit spread as discussed earlier in this chapter.

Put Credit Spread: Sell 23450 PE and Buy 23350 PE for hedge.

The maximum you can gain from this trade is (109 − 70.75) × 25 = ₹956. You will get this amount even if Nifty closes above 23450.

And if your view is wrong, the maximum you would lose is: (100 × 25) − 956 = ₹1,544.

You will start losing money only if Nifty falls below 23410. If your research was wrong — it is better to admit and accept the ensuing loss. But if you continue to believe that your research is right and should reward you — and that the temporary fall is due to a false trigger then you can fire-fight the situation as follows:

1. Take another put credit spread but at a lower level and with a bigger lot size.
2. Take a fresh call credit spread but at a higher level and with a bigger lot size.

For Example:

Case 1: Sell 8 lots of 23000 PE and buy 8 lots of 22800 PE Figure 10.9.

You can see in Figure 10.9 that the risk-reward is heavily skewed to the max-loss side. Because we went farther away from the money (OTM), the premiums were lower to compensate a small loss we need to take a higher risk.

Maximum profit: ₹1,560 / Maximum loss: ₹38,440 / Margin required: ₹1.339 lakhs.

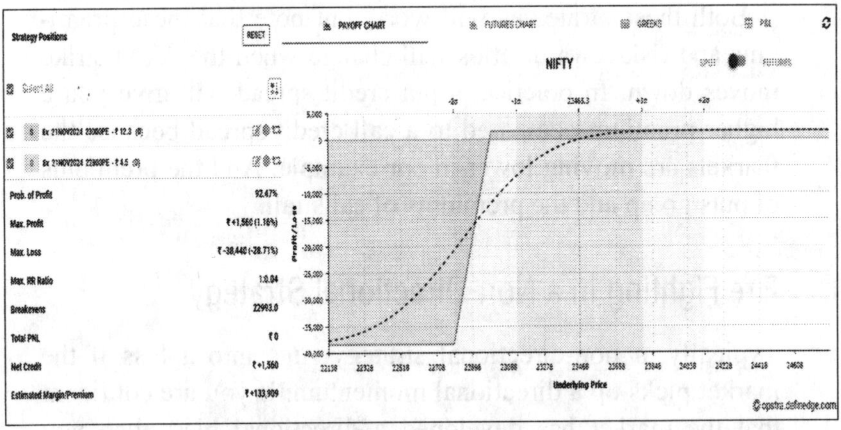

Figure 10.9: **Risk Payoff Diagram for the Fire-Fighting Strategy**

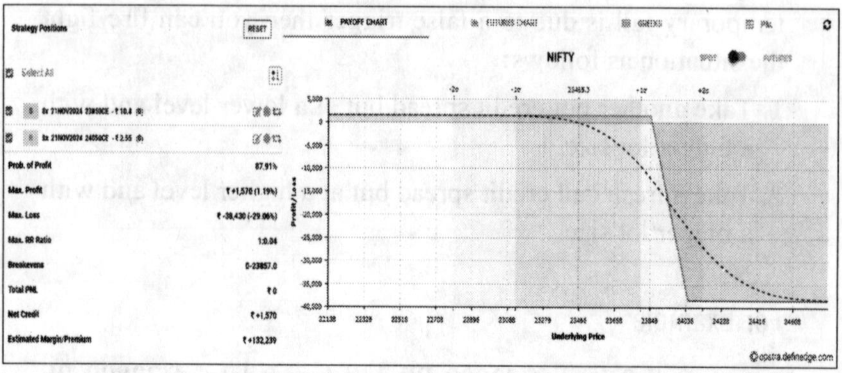

Figure 10.10: **Risk Payoff Diagram for the Fire-Fighting Strategy**

Case 2: Sell 8 lots of 23850 CE and buy 8 lots of 24050 CE (*see* Figure 10.10).

Again, the risk-reward is skewed to the maximum loss side. That's because in this method also we are going further away from the ATM.

Maximum profit: ₹1,570 / Maximum loss: ₹38,430 / Margin required: ₹1.322 lakh.

Both these strategies will work, but note that these premiums and risk-reward ratios will change when the ATM strike moves down. In practice, a put credit spread will give you a higher premium compared to a call credit spread because the markets are moving lower in our example. And the premiums of puts go up and the premiums of calls fall.

Fire Fighting in a Non-Directional Strategy

Typically, a non-directional strategy runs into a loss if the market picks up a directional momentum. If you are confident that the market has developed a directional bias, then you should exit your position even at a loss and not hang on to it in the hope that the trade would somehow turn out right.

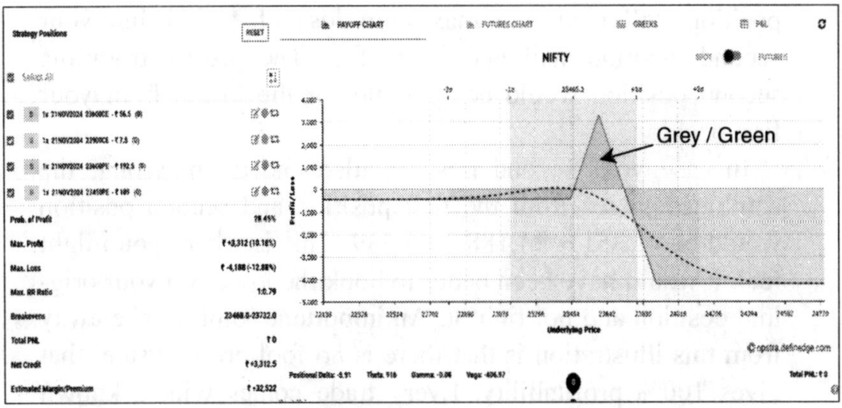

Figure 10.11:- **Risk Payoff Diagram for the Fire-Fighting Strategy**

However, if you think the market has only temporarily broken your expected range, then you can deploy a modified iron-fly or a modified iron-condor to capitalize on the situation.

Going by the example cited above:

- Sell 23600 CE & PE; and
- Buy 23900 CE and 23450 PE.

The maximum profit will be ₹3,312 while the maximum loss will be ₹4,188. The trade will be profitable if Nifty manages to close in the range (denoted in grey color) between 23468 to 23732 in this particular case (*see* Figure 10.11).

This new position is taken along with your existing position, so you should know how to calculate the combined maximum profit and loss. Let me explain it in detail. If you refer to Figure 10.5, the maximum profit was ₹3,649 and the maximum loss was ₹1,351. The losses of ₹1,351 are applicable only if Nifty trades above 23595 and as per the new fire-fighting position you have taken — the maximum loss of ₹438 is applicable below 23468 and a loss of ₹4,188 above 23732. If Nifty manages to expire at 23600 your original position will incur the maximum loss of ₹1,351 but your second position will end in profits. The profits from the second position would compensate for the losses from your first position.

In case your second position also ended up wrong, the combined losses from the first position and second position would be ₹1,351 + ₹4,188 = ₹5,539. This is where you might feel, it would have been better to book the losses on your original position and not fight it. An important point to take away from this illustration is that there is no fool-proof system that gives 100% profitability. Every trade comes with a known risk, so it is highly recommended to do the correct research before jumping in.

Professionals sell naked options to do the fire-fighting but I would not recommend that you do so — that's because it is an unlimited loss strategy and could blow your account to shreds.

Our priority is to save our original trade capital, even if we run into the permissible pre-set loss.

3 Rules for Trading

Rule1: Never lose money in a trade.

Rule 2: Even if you lose money, stay alive to fight (trade) another day.

Rule 3: Even if you forget Rule-1, do not forget Rule-2.

Sometimes our position may be running into a loss and we feel it would be a good idea to carry it overnight. Unless you are absolutely confident, do not take losses overnight. **Surviving to fight another day is more important than your ego not allowing you to accept a loss.**

Again, the most experienced traders get only 6 trades out of 10 right. The other four trades would go wrong and they book their losses. If they choose not to cut their loss, it could well grow and may even wipe out their capital.

At all times our priority is to protect the original ₹20 lakh in the G-Secs / GOI bonds. Intraday losses should be handled from the funds in your trading account, or could be borrowed from the emergency fund. (we will discuss emergency fund in Chapter 13). Never ever should your trading losses force you to liquidate the original ₹20 lakh GOI bonds.

You should always look at trading as a business. Running a successful business requires skills, intelligence, money management, risk management, and a bit of optimism. Opportunities in the trading business arise from market conditions. Sometimes the market could be benevolent, while most times it would be frugal. So a bit of optimism will go a long way in building a successful trading career.

If you are running into losses you need to hope that markets are going to be better tomorrow than they were today. Only then will you have the will power to book the small loss today in order to survive for the next day's trade. In the initial stages the number of losses may be higher than the number of wins — but you need to keep up your confidence and take necessary steps to perfect your trade craft.

11

How to Design a Trading Strategy Based on Your Risk Profile

WHAT MATTERS WHEN IT COMES TO TRADE EXECUTION is your profile as an individual. Remember the dialogue by Tom Cruise in the movie, "Top Gun Maverick"— "It's not the plane that's important, it's the pilot."

This makes perfect sense even in options trading. That's because the emotional make-up of each individual is different. Your belief system, risk profile and your education / training since childhood all have a huge role to play.

How each individual deals with money is called financial intelligence. And this depends on what you were taught during childhood. Some parents say, "Money is the root of all evil," "Rich people don't have peace of mind," "Staying poor shows you have down-to-earth character," etc.

This is how many people think of money. Money, however, does not think about you that way. It's just a piece of paper that offers you something in exchange.

When you enter a trade, your psychology impacts your actions and thus affects your trading performance and outcomes. If you have a balanced mindset, the job is half done. If you know how to correct your mindset, you will get there soon. But if you do not know what needs to be done then there is no way out.

Options trading is a self-employment business. It is a fair system which will reward you for being right, but bleed you if you go wrong. It is like any other business or job, but not like a 9-to-5 type of job.

Trading will not give you more money simply because you spend more time on the job, unlike, say, IT consultancy where companies bill their clients on headcount multiplied by the number of hours. You will not get more money by logging more work hours trading, or stretching your working life.

Trading is not a salaried job; it is a skill-based job. You need to be an expert and also know where, when and how to use your expertise. A normal job gives you an assurance of a pay-check at the end of every month. You are also entitled for some days of leave with pay every month and also get a plethora of benefits like travel, housing, dearness allowance. Some jobs provide you lifelong pension, too.

Trading is no match for that; there are no assured payouts, no allowances, no pension — and the leave of absence will always result in a loss of pay! You are your own boss; you need to decide how much to earn from the markets and then decide to do its equivalent effort.

The big positive aspect of trading *versus* a salaried job is the upper limit of the income you can earn. In trading, your earnings are not capped here, you get what you are worth. You must become your own mentor, pat yourself when outperforming, and pull up your socks when underperforming.

A doctor will only succeed if he is able to cure the patient. A lawyer will succeed only if he wins cases for his clients. An engineer will succeed only if he fixes the problem at hand. Similarly, a trader will succeed only if his research is accurate, and its execution is spot on.

In all the above examples the professionals concerned were put through intense education and apprenticeship before becoming successful. As an options trader you need to largely self-educate and commit yourself to apprenticeship before expecting a decent income.

This book was written with the objective of offering you that discipline And its assumption is that you will spend your first three years in on-the-job training.

In options trading, there are infinite number of combinations you could design by changing strike prices, adding trading legs, and varying the lot sizes. Literally, any style of payoff chart can be designed, deployed and executed. The use of an online strategy builder will help you get a better idea of the payoff chart, breakeven prices, maximum profit, maximum loss, etc.

There are some websites that even accurately calculate the time decay and the price changes by percentage drop / increase in volatility, etc.

Direction plus time plus volatility, in addition to the types of strategies used, further multiply the possible combinations. So there is every chance of getting carried away.

And when the markets swing very quickly your situation might be like that of a deer caught in a car's headlights. It may be impossible to think fast and clearly on what strategy or fire-fighting techniques you need to use in such situations.

My personal advice is to keep things simple. Once you keep practicing you will get the hang of it and most likely can stop depending on an online website to calculate the maximum profit / maximum loss figures.

Every trade should be designed and planned to give you profits. If there is no clear path to profits, or you can't find any trading opportunity — stay away. Always remember the money is already working for you *via* the GOI bonds that you've pledged.

When people start trading, they feel often almost compelled to take a trade every day. Such an approach results in over-trading or booking unplanned losses. Trading can't be instinct- or gut feel-driven, contrary to what most people think. Trading has to be well-planned and executed with rigorous discipline. Only veteran traders, namely traders with more than over twenty years of experience, can depend on their instincts.

Traders who make money just by following their inner voice or instincts don't realize it is in fact luck they are banking on. And luck can run out any time.

Profitable trading must be engineered to perfection; luck might help you a bit. But your design should pay you even if luck is not on your side.

The most under appreciated factor is good research. Most traders do not do sufficient home-work before trading. The probability theory will work for you during options trading — but nothing can ever be a substitute for your own independent research.

I maintain a trading journal and make explicit notes of where I made mistakes. If things go according to plan, it means business as usual and it never gets mentioned in my journal.

On the other hand, my failures or mistakes get written down every day and this has helped me better my trading system. I did not notice such changes in a week or even one month but after the first year it gave me lot of action points to work on.

Trading has considerable similarity with the theory of economics. Economics says that while resources are limited desires remain ever unlimited. Now, since, all our desires cannot be fulfilled we will have to let go a few to prioritize those that are more important.

Similarly, there could be multiple set-ups we can trade every single day, but only one or two of those will be the ideal ones. The courage to let go of non-profitable trading set-ups in favor of profitable ones is a special skill.

This also brings in the concept of opportunity cost — namely, what else could our money be doing instead of the current trade we have taken! Trading is also a game of scarcity, so we need to keep our cool in order to extract the maximum juice from every position we take.

A good trading strategy will have the following components:

1. Entry criteria;
2. Exit criteria;
3. Solid rationale;
4. Visibility on maximum profit;
5. Visibility on maximum loss and stop loss;
6. Time duration;
7. Risk management;
8. Position sizing
9. Assumptions.

Let us discuss each of the above points in detail.

Entry Criteria

Options trading has a lot of similarity with cricket. Even in his prime Sachin Tendulkar did not hit every ball to the boundary; he would wait for the appropriate ball to play his big shot. If the ball was dangerous, he would either leave it alone or defend it.

Similarly, successful trading does not mean you take on every possible trade. You should initiate a trade only when conditions are favorable. Waiting for the right set-up / opportunity is a great virtue in trading.

Most newcomers to trading may not immediately understand this, that's why the cricket analogy. Had he tried to hit every ball to the boundary, Sachin would have needlessly risked his wicket, or run out of energy. And most likely he would have scored fewer runs than he actually did in his career.

Similarly, if you try to take each and every possible trade available, you will either lose money or risk burn-out due to heavy stress. You will end up more miserable than before.

Defining entry criteria is easier said than done. You need to narrow down strategies that will give you an edge. This is something that you need to identify for yourselves. Edge is that which gives you an advantage over other market participants — it could be education, research, information, or speed of execution.

It may take many months or years to perfect your edge — but it's still worth developing one. You could start with six to seven types of trading set-ups, and then narrow it down to one or two by the end of three years.

Personally I have only one trading setup, and I know exactly when to enter the trade with it. Sometimes the opportunity does not knock every day so the waiting period can be really tiring. Nevertheless I enter a trade only if conditions are favorable — this reduces the chances of failure by up to 80%.

Exit Criteria

This is even more difficult than formulating an entry criteria because we need to have a clear idea when to square off, namely exit, our position. Since this is at a future date / time — so most of the time our vision will obviously not be that clear.

It is like playing chess; we need to calculate the opponent's next three moves and have a plan in place for countering each one. It takes effort, mathematical analysis and assessing probabilities. If it feels too much a task for you, let me stop you here!

Trading will only reward the top 5% of the participants. If you wish to be on top, you need to upskill yourself to be in that elite 5% club. The only advantage you have here is that it does not ask your previous work experience, degree certificate or work permit. Anyone can get into trading, but only the skilled will survive.

Luck does play a role in profits, so does risk. Assuming that luck will be always with you is a mistake. Your skills, on the other hand, will stay with you forever. Of course, skills also require constant upgradation.

The option strategies we discussed in the previous chapters discussed the concepts of maximum profit and maximum loss. There is no compulsion to hold on to the trade till the very last second on the expiry day.

You are free to exit whenever you are comfortable doing so. That timing is completely up to you.

Solid Rationale

Whether a trade works out or not, you need to know the reason why you got into the trade to begin with; that is what I am referring to as solid rationale. You could be wrong 50% of the time — but that's okay so long as you had a logic to start with.

Rationale, logic or intelligence comes from a knowledge of the system, theories, experience and exposure. Rationale comes from having a view and then designing a trading plan to go with it.

Most importantly, if the market has proven you wrong it is better to accept that and exit. Do not try and fight the market — it does not even know who you are!

My personal accuracy is just above the 50% mark, just above a coin toss random probability. Each of the trade that I take is taken with full conviction (the why part). If I feel the market is going against me, I look for opportunities to exit and fight another day.

Visibility on Maximum Profit

It is hard but before you enter a trade you need to know what is the maximum possible profit you can earn from it. If you don't know the goal, you might have to settle with whatever the market gives you.

In discussing the strategies in the previous chapter we looked at the maximum profit you could get from each trade. That will happen only in the ideal situation, in practice things may go sideways also.

To start with, it may be difficult to assess the maximum profit because you might not really know the potential of your existing positions. Option selling *via* credit spreads will give you greater visibility. Starting from there, you might venture into unlimited profit strategies too — in reality, of course, there are no unlimited gains. Every option instrument expires, i.e. it is limited by time. So even if you had an unlimited profit strategy, its run will get checked by the passage of time.

If you set your expectations correctly, you would know when and how much profits to book.

Visibility on Maximum Loss and Stop Loss

Since the strategies we have discussed in the earlier chapters are ones with pre-defined limited profits and limited losses, you need not worry about the maximum losses that could occur. Such strategies automatically take care of the worst case for you. Whereas option strategies like "short straddles", "short strangles", and "naked short selling" come with unlimited losses and could even wipe out your capital.

Since you are just starting, I understand how difficult it is to set the stop loss correctly. Booking losses may feel very painful, but as you become a professional trader you will embrace the idea that a small loss is better than a huge one. The strategies presented in this book, such as credit and debit spreads, short iron fly, and short iron condor have in-built maximum loss criteria. If you feel the market is going against your strategy, and you would like to preserve your capital, there is no harm in exiting your trade even prematurely. You need not wait for the maximum loss to be realized.

In the real world you might chase a trending market and may use unlimited profit/unlimited loss strategies such as naked option buying and selling. This requires a preventive stop to save you from losing the capital.

Stop loss can be considered as the penalty you pay for getting your research wrong. If it hurts you bad, you would realize how much you need to improve.

For any unlimited profit / loss strategy it is good to use a stop loss so that your capital is protected and you live to fight another day. I have seen traders placing a stop loss at about 20% to 30% of the option's premium value depending on the circumstance. For example, if the BUY entry price was ₹100, the stop loss could be ₹80 or ₹70. This means that if the option's premium drops below the stop loss, system automatically exits the trade and preserves the remaining capital.

Time Duration

The time spent in a trade is very important because we are trading options. And options come with expiry dates. Were we trading stocks, we can have the mindset to wait out the losing phase since that wait does not have a time tag attached to it.

In India, Nifty50 index options expire every Thursday, and Sensex options expire Tuesdays. This brings in urgency! We need to become good at taking quick decisions in order to improve our profitability.

Also no one really cares if you hold the position for the entire period of 5 days, or just 5 minutes. How much you are able to extract from your strategy is what matters.

Before entering a trade, you need to figure out how long you need to stay in it to achieve the profits you have in mind. This period need not be 100% accurate — a broad idea will do. And if it exceeds the time allotted, you need to have a backup plan too.

In my experience never has there been a situation where two of my trades lasted the exact same time. Like a fingerprint, each trade is different, and that's because the markets do not behave the same way every time.

Risk Management

The real name of this game is risk management and not options trading. If you recollect, options were invented as a hedging instrument and we are taking the counter position to the hedger.

That exposes us to risk because we do not have the backing of an investment if our position goes wrong. Thus, each and every time we need to design a plan to beat the hedger. You need to outsmart that guy and you should enter the battle only if you know you can win. This is not the battle for Troy where you will be remembered even if you fail.

Seriously, nobody cares if you lose, or if your capital is wiped out. But so long as you stay alive and kicking, you stand a chance to earn a name!

Risk management has two components:

1. Estimating the risk correctly and charging a premium to cover that risk.
2. Exiting the position with a minimum loss if the risk is real.

To be profitable in options trading, you need to think like an insurance company which has an underwriter to evaluate the risk and then increase or reduce the premium of the insurance policy accordingly. If the underwriter feels the risk cannot be covered, the insurer simply stops issuing the policy.

The options trader has to similarly assess the risk, estimate the fair value of the strike, and only then place a trade. If the premium is too high, it does not make sense to buy that option. Similarly, if the premium is too low, you should not short-sell it.

When we take a trade, we are speculating against the hedger and it is unreasonable to think we will always win. A sensible strategy would be to cut your losses when you go wrong. Every professional trader does that and you need not feel bad when markets humble you; it is all a part of the game.

Position Sizing

We have a base capital of ₹20 lakh. In the examples considered above, the maximum margin that's required per lot for a credit spread was ₹0.20 lakh. Which means with your capital you can trade up to 100 lots at the same time.

What is it going to be? How much lots would you trade??

This depends on your personal risk profile. There is no one pill for all patients or all ailments. You need to find the right balance for yourself.

Assumptions

The least talked about aspects of a trading plan are its prerequisites or variables you had priced in. You might have entered the trade making some assumptions and considering some variables as constants. Every trader does that and it is not wrong to assume a few things, but we need to be alert if these assumptions are changing drastically. Financial markets are very complex but a simple news could change the entire narrative and chances are it could mess up your trades.

For example, you might have decided to go long on Nifty for the current weekly expiry and entered into a bullish debit spread. Things were going your way and then the RBI Governor makes an appearance and hikes the repo rates by 35 basis points. You had assumed the interest rate would not change in the current week, but it did. Evaluating your positions and then exiting or adjusting to accommodate the change in variables is better. If we do not adapt to the new development, our positions may run into losses

What I am trying to say is that we need to always stay alert to these "plan busters" and react accordingly. After you get into a trade and the variables change beyond a level — it is safer to exit at a loss than stay in the hole.

~

Options are derivative instruments; their pricing is largely dependent on the underlying. For example, the price of the 23400 CALL option is highly dependent on Nifty's current price of 23462. If Nifty goes up another 100 points, the value of 23400 CE will also rise but not as much as by 100 points.

Apart from the direction (delta), time value (theta), volatility (vega), interest rate (rho) are all variables that affect the price of 23400 CE. All these variables change dynamically with every tick, and as a professional trader your trades should have enough leeway to accommodate these changes.

One thing that is guaranteed is that you cannot set a monthly expectation or target. You may be able to decide a range of income you wish to generate every month, but being stubborn about meeting that target is foolishness.

The market conditions change from time to time, and our trade entry/exit points may vary. The time duration of the trades may vary. The news flow, events or result declarations will change market dynamics. This is the main reason we cannot predict with 100% accuracy what our daily, weekly, or monthly profits would be.

However, if you set a predefined target and under achieve it by the last week of the trade, there's the risk that you might start over trading. You might also become frustrated and miserable and deviate from your normal trading style to take on additional risk.

Think of the markets as a gold mine. We keep digging every day. Some days we get a good discovery, but the other days we just collect rubble. We cannot overdo the digging and risk our personal health and safety — the number one priority is to stay alive so that we survive to go on digging the next day.

Summary

To summarize this chapter: the trading strategy that you need to use should be designed by you. No outsider or research analyst can help you do so. You must design it yourself.

All you need is a computer, internet, a broker account and some funds to start this business. Your success depends entirely on your ability to follow your trading plan every day, day after day. Even if it takes some time to design and implement your trading plan — so be it. No need to hurry; it's more important to do it right!

Also, focus on the rationale part; every time you are proven wrong — investigate why. If you dig deeper, you will uncover a new variable, a new financial concept or some interesting data points. Take the effort to read and digest that — one bite at a time.

Section

~

4

12
~
Start with Paper Trading

PAPER TRADING IS A METHOD which gives you the same experience as real trades but without having to spend real money. That means you do not need actual funds to paper trade — the profit or loss you incur are notional, only on paper. It's like a pilot training and perfecting his / her skills on a flight simulator, without risking either his / her life or a real combat aircraft.

The Opstra website provides this facility and I strongly recommend you try out its free features. A maximum of two paper trades can be done at a time and it will show you near real-time profit/loss for the entire duration of your trade.

Even the best technical analyst in the world will not have accuracy above 70%. If you are stepping into this domain, it is important that you accept and acknowledge this inherent limitation. Trading with the expectation of 100% accuracy each time will only lead to frustration, panic and even psychological breakdown.

Paper trades are a solution for assessing the accuracy of your analysis. To start with, take 20 paper trades, note down the exact time, price and reason why you took each trade.

After those 20 trades, count your wins. If you are below five, you need to prepare some more before you trade with real money.

If you wins are between 5 to 10, it's an average score. Most traders would fall in this range. This means you still need to perfect your timing and edge.

If you score between 10 and 15 wins — you are an absolute professional! It is only matter of time before money starts flowing into your account.

If your win score is 15+, then you are a genius.

Let me assume your score is between 10 and 15, and if you are still not confident to take a trade — you should continue to paper trade to 50 count or 100 count till you build enough confidence.

Why Paper Trading is Important

During a trade your position swings from profit to loss, and back into profit several times. Paper trading gives you an opportunity to analyze such swings with a clear mind since no real money is involved.

The same experience is available in real trades but when you see real money losses emotions come into play which can impact your decisions. Anxiety, stress and fear of losses often force traders to exit trades at the wrong time, leaving them even more miserable. Paper trades will solve that issue to an extent.

Chart Reading

Charts form the foundation of technical analysis. A chart captures the price of a stock or index between 9.15 AM to 3.30 PM every day. Thus, there are 375 minutes of trading every day. If you plot the chart keeping the time frame as 1-minute, you will get 375 candlesticks. Each candlestick shows how the price moved during that one minute. You can even set the time frame for 5 minutes, 15 minutes, one hour, one day, one week, etc. Shorter time frames are used if you are trading for the ultra short-term duration; for example, intraday traders use the 5-minute and 15-minute time frame. Medium time frames are used by swing traders and positional traders, for example, 1-day, 1-week, etc. Traders monitoring sectoral changes use longer time frames such as 1-week, 1-month, etc.

There is a truck-load of information available for interpretation from the price actions depicted in charts 12.1, 12.2 and 12.3. Each candle has a story to tell, so do the combinations of candle sticks.

Price action and candlestick patterns are beyond the scope of this book and I request you to familiarize yourself with them as soon as possible.

Figure 12.1: **A 5-Minute Chart of the Nifty**

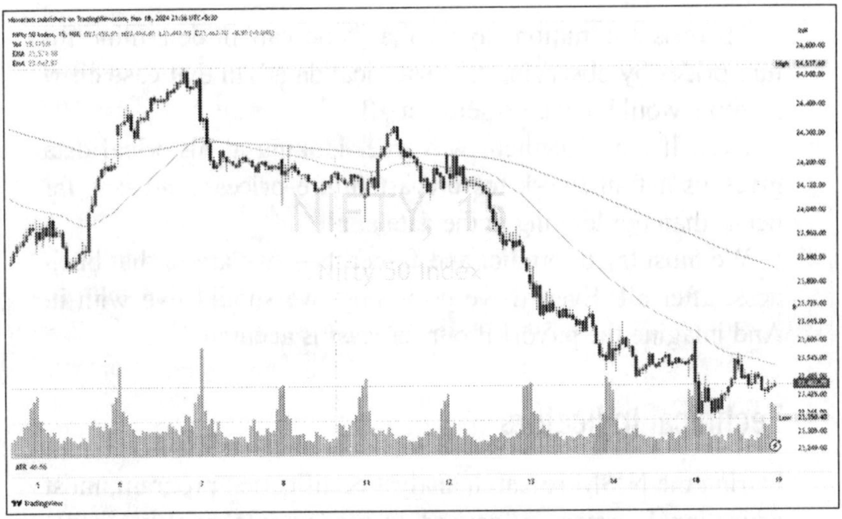

Figure 12.2: **A 15-Minute Chart of Nifty**

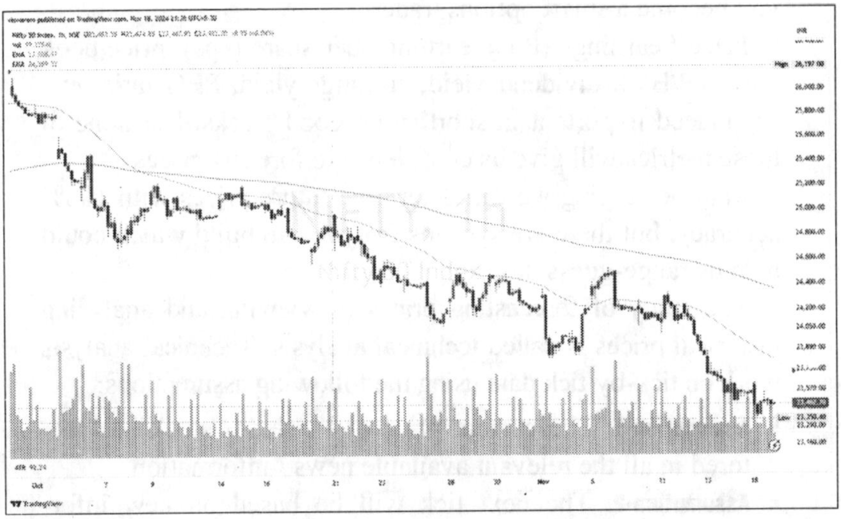

Figure 12.3: **A 1-Hour Chart of Nifty**

There is a common saying that "one cannot determine future prices by observing the historical data." In that case chart patterns would make no sense at all.

Even if that statement was true, looking at historical data gives us a framework to forecast future prices. And it is far better than not looking at the data at all.

We must try to predict and forecast — we are in that business, after all. Even if we go wrong, we should live with it. And imagine the payoff if our forecast is accurate?

Technical Indicators

During the NISM research analyst certification program, most educational content is focused on fundamental analysis, company ratios and valuation metrics. Although these skills are very important for stock selection — they are unlikely to help you become a smart options trader.

Price / earnings (P/E), earnings per share (eps), price/book value (P/BV), dividend yield, earnings yield, PEG ratio, etc. are indeed important in shortlisting good stocks. But none of these metrics will give us confidence to forecast prices.

I am not saying we can determine future prices with 100% accuracy, but there are systems that we can build which could help us range-guess it.

The study of forecasting prices by viewing and analyzing historical prices is called technical analysis. Technical analysts work on tick-by-tick data using the following assumptions:

- **Assumption-1:** The current price of the index/stock has factored in all the relevant available news / information.
- **Assumption-2:** The next tick will be based on new information.

Once these ticks are plotted on a chart, we can see the price:

1. Rising;

2. Falling;
3. Staying at the same level;
4. Making an abrupt gap-up;
5. Making an abrupt gap-down;
6. Rising, staying at a zone, and then breaking down;
7. Falling, taking rest and then surging back up.

The price does not always move in a straight line, it keeps plotting interesting patterns every day. To become a good options trader, you need to fall in love with the study of charts.

Over a period you will be able to memorize chart and candlestick patterns. You will be also able to guess the next move with a fair level of accuracy. Although nobody can predict prices with 100% accuracy, looking at the chart is a better idea than not doing so.

We are not guessing the future price of the index/stock to directly make money out of it. Our job as an option trader is to handle our positions when the market moves. Let me try to explain this with an example.

Suppose the stock price of XYZ is currently ₹120. And based on our analysis we expect the prices to go up to, say, ₹140. The only way this can be handled is to buy at ₹120 and sell at ₹140, and the difference becomes the profit.

Options traders could deploy a bullish credit spread to handle this trade. If the stock price of XYZ is at ₹120 and is making a move to ₹140, we can sell a 120PUT option and buy a 110PUT option. Our trade will then remain profitable so long as the price stays above ₹120. In case the price is not stable above ₹120, we could exit our trade prematurely to limit any possible losses.

Option traders need not predict the market direction to make money; an appropriate timely response to the market's move is enough.

The bed rock of technical indicators is based on the concept of support and resistance levels. In a nutshell, supports are formed below the current trading price, while resistances are formed above the current trading price.

Support and resistance are points of interest because the stock or index has already earlier spent considerable time at those levels. Technical analysts monitor these levels to determine if the trend will continue or reverse from these areas. If the stock breaches a support level, the analyst usually goes bearish. Correspondingly, if the stock takes out a resistance level, the analyst will look out for bullish opportunities.

Markets do not move in the same direction all the time — there will always be reversals, pull backs or breaks.

The encircled areas in Figure 12.4 are points of interest where Nifty showed some inertia in its movement. For me these are the support points when the current price is above these levels.

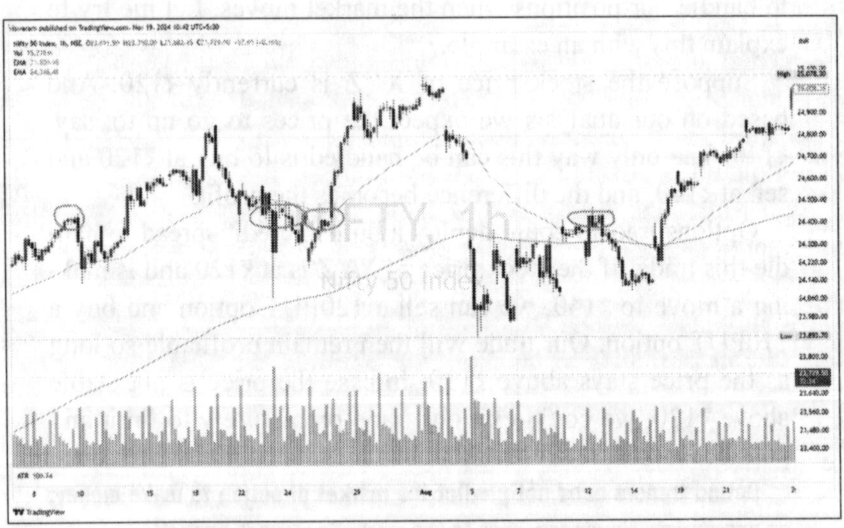

Figure 12.4: **Points of Interests Encircled**

When the price breaks down from a support area and moves further down, then that broken support level becomes a new resistance level. Thus if Nifty were to move back up — this level will resist, or test, the upmove.

All these are virtual levels that we mark on the chart and there is no guarantee that such support and resistance levels will always work as expected. What Nifty does, it does; our intention is to just record that on a chart.

These areas on the chart need not be similar for every trader, so there are no fixed points or levels *per se*. You and I might be looking at the same chart and have totally different levels, and that is perfectly fine.

Supports and resistances are the simplest and most powerful technical indicators available. Simple, because these are just horizontal lines that we all can draw on the price chart. Powerful because these levels act as friction zones that stop, or reverse, a high-speed move.

Let's suppose Nifty is falling very heavily on a news event. Often the first thing traders do is panic and square off all outstanding positions. A technical trader can look at the charts and find the nearest support area. And then decide to exit, or hold on, to the trade if this support area breaks.

Most times violent news-driven or event-driven market reactions turn out to be minor short term blips. If we time our entry and exit without proper analysis — the market will take out our protective stop losses. The best advice is to watch for the nearest support and resistance zones, and place your stop loss accordingly so that you are not ousted by false triggers.

Other technical indicators you use in addition to these is totally up to you. You might have to take a course or read multiple books to learn about these indicators.

Only if you understand 10 to 15 technical indicators will you be able to decide which ones to use on different occasions.

By definition, technical indicators are supposed to guide you to take a concrete decision, whether on the direction of the trade, or its timing.

Most of these indicators follow the price and are hence called lagging indicators. There are a few leading indicators as well though their accuracy is up for debate.

These are all in your learning arsenal and you can try around things. Most of the technical indicators are free and if you like coding then definitely checkout Trading View's pine script library.

You might have heard the saying, "Do not try to time the market." Well, that is for the average folks out there. It was popularized by mutual fund companies to get more people to invest *via* systematic investment plans (SIP).

I strongly suggest you to start timing the markets. Try to predict where the market is headed, and the rationale behind it. Only then can you earn the right to be in this field. No matter what mutual fund managers tell you — they do try to time the markets and also trade their bias, i.e. market view.

You can only have a trading strategy if you have a bias or a view, whether directional or non-directional. If you have no view — then you obviously cannot take a trade. The issue is that we cannot trade on the basis of hope or prayer; we need something that is more tangible to back us. And that science is what we derive from our own research.

"Own research" need not be purely technical, you can also have a fundamental view. Fundamentals, too, move the market. The reason people buy a stock is because they expect it will give good returns. So, in effect, investors pay for future valuations.

Technical analysis cannot give you such estimates of future valuations. It is just a mathematical price modelling based on the data we already have. Most importantly, our research can also go wrong. Every time we go wrong, we need to spend more time to analyze the mistake. That will help us find new snippets of information that we did not price in. And over time our research will have sharper focus and greater clarity.

Imagine you are working as a fund manager of a big AMC. You are given ₹10,000 crore to invest or trade based on your research. What will you do?

This would give sleepless nights to most of us. Why? Because a lot of investors will be impacted if we go wrong; they might lose their funds and we may get crucified.

Now imagine you have ₹10,000 to invest / trade. Would it really trouble you? Or, will you have the feeling, "Ah, its only ₹10,000, even if it goes to zero it is not a big deal."

My point is be it ₹10,000 or ₹10,000 crore, the investment / trading decision must be based on thorough research. Your research should not be based on your intuition, but on solid analysis. And if you go wrong even after that — it's okay. That is where our stop loss comes into play and enables us to exit safely with relatively modest and bearable loss.

Sometimes when we manage lesser money, we may not have great seriousness to put in hours of hard work into research and learning. People are generally motivated by more money. That is why the same employee will work harder (at least for a while) if more money is offered.

For your trading career it is very important that you take research seriously. Even if you were not that good in mathematics, now is the right time to learn. Trading is not easy or simple — it is difficult, but if you have done your analysis correctly you will have more control over the outcomes!

13

~

Backtest and Forward Test Your Strategies

IN AN EARLIER CHAPTER WE TALKED ABOUT acquiring an "edge." An edge is something specific which gives you a clear advantage *vis-a-vis* other traders.

To see if your edge generates money consistently you need to back-test it. This means you need to find periods in the past when this strategy was deployed and what the outcome was.

There are many online websites — both free and paid — that offer this facility. The best place to start is on Trading View, which is a charting platform.

There are many back-testing websites / software available but most of them are paid services. And there is a good reason why they are a premium offering; the complexity of the data crunching done by the software is immense. Nobody can offer that much of computer hardware processing free of cost.

AlgoTest and TradeTron are two excellent platforms if you are looking for a paid service. Whatever amount you pay for either of these websites is worth its weight in gold. This is because it may take you a lifetime if you were to manually crunch the data. I am a big fan of algorithmic trading due to the speed at which it can punch the trades. I use the TradingView platform for directional trades and AlgoTest platform for non-directional trades.

Wait a minute, am I talking about full automation?

Absolutely not! It is too early to automate things that you have no fair idea about. But you could note down these triggers over a period and monitor how, or if, your edge actually worked out.

Automation is only possible if the trades you intend to take work out properly in a manual setup. Automation is not intelligence; it is a computerized system to speed up a manual process. Thus, for example, if the strategies you employ manually are loss making ones — there is a 100% certainty that they will still make losses *via* the automation route too.

Backtesting is the process of testing your trade logic on actual historical data. You could write down your trade logic into an algorithm and use a professional service like AlgoTest to test the outcome during some past period. You could specify the exact dates you wish to test, or even test it for a full year. Typically all backtest software provides the following information:

1. Overall profit;
2. Number of trades;
3. Average profit per trade;
4. Win percentage;
5. Loss percentage;
6. Maximum profit in a single trade;
7. Maximum loss in a single trade;
8. Maximum drawdown;
9. Reward to risk ratio;
10. Returns to maximum drawdown ratio.

The purpose of any back test is to fine tune your strategy to make it more efficient. You should be aware that the actual execution will have slippages due to bid/ask spread and liquidity. You should use the back test only as a reference, and not depend on it entirely.

If you do not wish to use paid software for back-testing, you can do a forward-test. I assume if you are planning to trade as a full-time job, then it requires hours of time being spent in front of charts, trading terminal, etc.

You can note down your entry / exit criteria on paper when you see them and then analyze how it performed that day. Over a period of, say, six months, you will have enough data to assess the forward-test capabilities. Forward testing is similar to live trade execution and can be automated *via* AlgoTest. Instead of connecting the broker and executing it live, you configure a bot to run the exact trades as in the production environment.

In real time you can watch your profit/loss, current positions, entry/exit triggers, and the exact time-stamp of orders. The advantage of a forward test is that it will help you to monitor things objectively as no money is involved. The only limitation is that you could run only one trade a day and to get sizeable data to work with, you might have to wait for 6 to 12 months.

Testing whether *via* by coding or manually will give you immense sense of security and confidence. It will also reassure you to stick with your plan and trade accordingly. If you have some computer or IT background it will go a long way in this section. It is not unwise to even buy a paid back-test software either.

Again reiterating the fact that even the best trader in the world only achieves between 60% to 70% win rates. 50+% win rate in itself is a good score, you might be in the elite 20% trader group in case you are achieving just over 50% win rates.

Even if you have a 50% win rate, you can still outperform in this field if your risk-reward ratio is designed correctly. Getting 2x returns on wins and losing only 1x on failures will work out perfectly if you play the game long enough.

To make good money, it is enough that you be in the 81st percentile, or higher. But to be the best you need to be in 95th percentile, or higher. So here is a system that consistently evaluates your performance every time you play.

Taking a loss, or getting out from a losing trade, is nothing to be ashamed about. Occasional losses will keep you focused and humble. If we have a big winning streak, most often the decisions taken with respect to position sizing and the amount committed could really get out of control. A small loss which interrupts your winning streak will keep your ego in check and is much better than a huge loss that wipes out all the money you might have made in the previous six to nine months.

This is the only field where you need not submit an appraisal report to your boss, or please someone else to get a promotion. Your future is totally in your hands and it is a skill-based platform that rewards your merit. There are no politics or reservations here and you get what you are worth!

Sure, sometimes frauds do happen, but these are mostly associated with individual stocks, and not the indices. So by choosing index trading over stock trading — you are already in a sweet spot.

14

~

What is an Emergency Fund —and How Much Should You Have?

IT'S TIME NOW TO LOOK AT how to fund one's trading losses. Let's revisit the credit and debit strategy payout first to set the expectation.

Credit spread: adds funds to your ledger when the trade is initiated.

Debit spread: deducts funds from your ledger when the trade is initiated.

We need to have the flexibility to choose the kind of strategy that should be deployed for maximum earning from a situation. Your funds are locked and kept in GOI bonds, and at no time must that be touched, altered or redeemed.

This means we need to have some money available in cash to handle the debits or losses we run into. Ideally you need to have only 2% of the original capital in liquid cash, i.e. about ₹40,000 (₹0.40 lakh).

And you should make this the maximum permissible loss limit that you can hit at any time. If the cash ledger goes to zero — you must stop trading, and go back to the learning desk and dig deeper into research.

You will get paid approximately ₹11,666 as interest income every month. So you need to wait for four months before you get enough cash to top-up your ledger. Do not take another trade until your cash ledger is back at ₹0.40 lakh.

If you lose it again, you need to wait for another four months to top it up. And if you lose a third time as well — then it is better to call it quits.

If you have spent an entire year losing ₹1.2 lakh even after acquiring relevant knowledge, know-how and mindset to run this business — then the signs are obvious. You should seriously re-think your desire to be a trader.

After a year you would have earned ₹1.4 lakh in interest income while you had a net outgo of ₹1.2 lakh as losses *via* trading. Logically you have not lost that much money — but you would have lost a lot of time, effort and confidence.

None of the super-traders you see around now made it in a single year. They might have had years of losses before turning green. The rags-to-riches story looks very enticing for a Bollywood movie, but it seldom happens in real life.

Attrition is common in all fields, be it medicine, engineering, aerospace, academics, or even a regular day-job. People who quit need not be losers, they might be smarter than what the world thinks about them. They would have got the self-realization that they are not cut out for this job.

Trading is no exception; it is a normal business with the same probabilities of success. It is just that the people who become successful in trading get a disproportionate amount of attention and popularity, and spotlight which celebrities get.

If you came for that, most likely it won't inspire you to perform. If you came here to make it a profession, you can still get back on track. Re-read the trading plan chapter and see what went wrong before attempting your second year.

~

You also need to know how the losses or profits get debited or credited. Going back to the earlier example, suppose you got into a credit spread that has a maximum profit of ₹1,000 and a maximum loss of ₹1,500.

Then this ₹1,000 is instantly credited to your account. After a day you decide to square off the trades when the system showed a profit of ₹550. Since ₹1,000 was already paid to you, the ledger will now show a debit of ₹450 (1,000 – 550). This means you are richer by ₹550 at the end of this trade.

Coming to the debit spread example, if it showed a maximum profit of ₹1,200 and a maximum loss of ₹1,400, then ₹1,400 will get deducted from your ledger instantly. After a few days if you squared off the position at a profit of ₹400, then you will get paid ₹400+₹1,400 same day. On a net-to-net basis, you are richer by ₹400.

I hope you can yourself do the corresponding math on losses.

~

If trading is your only income, then you might need leeway for expenses also. This puts you under immense pressure to start generating revenue from the very first month. If you are not handling it right — it could turn out to be a disaster as well.

These days the monthly expense of a middle-class family could be about ₹40,000/- to ₹60,000/-. Generating this kind of income from trading alone will take a lot of expertise. There could be months of out-performance — but what about the low performing months?

This initial kitty of ₹40,000 is your first layer of defense. If your basket is rising in value, it will give you more freedom to try out new strategies. Suppose your new corpus is ₹60,000, it means you have a surplus of ₹20,000 that could fund your innovations or improvisations.

Even if things goes wrong, your morale is still not impacted. Most importantly, finding your edge in trading is more of an art than science — it will take you some time to discover and perfect your edge. Once you have found your elixir, it is just a matter of time. You just need to keep playing for a long time to create true wealth.

The additional revenue you generate can also go into equity or SIP, or another debt fund. Just make sure those are in the pledge list so that you can benefit from the power of compounding.

Also remember that just as how the index goes zig-zag, your trading account also will have ups and downs. It is not going to be a straight line, but if you have done the homework correctly — it might start looking like a straight line when you look at it on a higher time frame!

15 ~ Controlling Your Urge to Overtrade

THERE ARE NO BROWNIE POINTS for undertaking more trades in a year. If there were any awards it would be to find the trader who did the lowest number of trades and achieved the maximum ROI.

Every trade you get into will have an impact on your stress levels; that's because there is money involved. If you play football or cricket, you can relate to this, every game has a win / loss outcome. You feel good when you win and feel bad when you lose.

The stress that one goes through in order to perform in sports is similar; even people watching the game get nervous. But since there is no money involved, a lost game will not hurt you financially.

Trading has the same stress levels and excitement as a sports match. It also takes an additional toll on your emotions if you end up on the losing side. That's because not only have you lost the game, you have lost money, too.

This new add-on stress is similar to that faced by game-bettors and gamblers. Most people say trading is gambling for this reason — the feeling is the same. When you lose, you lose your confidence and also your capital.

The best way to stay calm and disciplined is to define your trading plan clearly. Only if the set-up criteria are matching perfectly should you commit to a trade. If the criteria are not met — do not trade. Let it pass, we know a perfect set-up will come in the next session.

I used to compile portfolio valuations daily, by doing this I could see how much my debt funds were appreciating every day. This small increase every day gave me the feeling that even if I do not trade — I am still earning interest. This really boosted my confidence and would allow to let an opportunity fly by if it was not meeting my trading set-up.

Your original capital parked in GOI bonds will give you a similar confidence. The market tends to pull people into its trap by seducing you with false narratives — it's way better not to pull the trigger. Choosing not to trade is a trade in itself.

Continuing with the analogy of a sports match, you might still remember the best game you would have played even though it may have been 10, 15 or 30 years back. Your best performance will always stay in your memory because you had a special feeling when it occurred.

On the other hand, the memories you accumulate in trading are the ones of failure or of the opportunities you missed. You might hardly remember how much money you made same month last year. That's because the feeling of missing out far exceeds the joy of wining.

Another important point here is that trading is exciting and adrenaline-pumping only for the newbie. For seasoned professionals, trading is just a job. Making more money seldom excites; people do not jump up in the air shouting "hurray" or "wow", etc.

Professionals get excited when their strategy works, not so much when it makes them a ton of money. Conversely, they get stressed when their planning fails, not when they see their position slipping into losses.

I am sure about the statement above. I wear a smartwatch that measures the stress levels during trading hours. Early in my trading journey my stress levels would spike above 33% to 66%, they would go from blue to yellow to orange.

My stress levels used to spike twice or thrice daily. These days I get only two to three spikes a week. If you have a smartwatch you should try it, too.

The records you have to break in trading are your own. You need not compare your trading profits with those of your friends, or some influencer. That is a recipe for disaster.

Again that is because even though there are lakhs of traders who trade options, hardly will we find any two with the same capital, the same set up, and same execution times. So if you compare your profits with someone else's, then it is like comparing oranges to apples.

You should also find time to compare your current month's performance with the previous month's. If possible, compare the recent three-month data. It will unlock more data points for improvements.

> *"I fear not the man who has practiced 10,000 kicks once, but I fear the man who has practiced one kick 10,000 times."* — Bruce Lee

In trading, too, if you practice one strategy multiple times you will become an expert at it with time. Usually, people advise you to learn broader aspects first and then specialize in one field — the entire education system is made that way.

Medicine, engineering and legal — they teach the basics first during graduation. Then they teach a specialization in post-graduation and finally you get into a niche segment for your PhD.

In options trading you can go the reverse; take your PhD first, then the post-graduation; and then your graduation. Focus on a niche segment first and become an expert at it, then learn the upstream systems in a broader way. This will help you steepen the learning curve, saving you time.

I used this tweak to save time and improve my learning speed. I just traded Nifty & BankNifty for three years using only a single strategy. Sometimes I waited so long for my entry setup to fall in place that I would fall asleep! Honestly, the good point was that the stress levels were lower and my hit rates kept improving.

Once you grow in confidence, you can spread your wings and handle a bunch of stocks, commodities or indices. That's because you know even if you have to start all over again, you still have a strategy that gave you the differentiating edge.

Finding and sharpening your edge and consistently improvising your strategies are required. It will be possible only if you have the right frame of mind, and for that you need to consistently win more than lose.

These days brokers come with a kill-switch, which is a feature to lock you off from taking trades. If you look at the yearly trading calendar, there are no continuous holidays or breaks — so if you need to take a vacation, you need to decide it for yourself. Sometimes a good break will rejuvenate you and bring down the work pressure and stress.

Also, while it's good to be profitable but don't be adamant about it. It is fine to take losses once in a while; it is also good for your humility. If you are stubborn about exiting every trade only at profit you might unnecessarily fire-fight a losing position, and make it worse. Also, your mental composure may get affected, further weakening your decision making.

On trading forums you can see multiple instances where a trader went into a ₹20+ lakh loss in a single day! That guy lost money not because he was not smart, but because his mindset was hacked by a recent trade's adverse outcome. He kept holding on to the losing trade hoping it will turn.

~

Section

~

5

16
~
The Marriage of Debt Funds with Your Trading Strategy

WE ARE NOW INTO THE MOST IMPORTANT CHAPTER of this book. In fact, this is what the book is all about — so let us take a deep dive into this topic.

Most newcomers to options trading business don't know much about pledging or funding their trading account from collateral. Most traders who make big money in this arena might be doing it using cash.

Only a small portion of active traders use collateral to fund their trading account; that's because doing so requires you to prioritize option selling over option buying.

And option buying has a 1500:1 leverage ratio against option selling. Let me explain how.

When Nifty was quoting at 23400, the farthest CE strike available was 26600 CE trading for ₹1.10 for an expiry on 21 November 2024.

Option Selling: To sell 1600 quantity of this option you would need ₹18.22 lakh in your account*.

---

* The margin requirements may change if the exchanges or the regulators revise the contract values and sizes.

The maximum profit you are going to get is 1.1 × 1600 = ₹1,760.

So you have a reward of 0.096% on the funds deployed. For most traders this does not seem attractive, it even looks dangerously low.

Option Buying: You can end up buying 16,56,000 quantity of this strike price with the same fund balance of ₹18.22 lakh.

Even if you manage to make ₹1 profit per unit on this trade, you can pocket ₹16.5 lakh, i.e. a 90% ROI on the funds deployed.

From a common trader's perspective, what would you choose? Trade 1700 quantity or trade with 16.5 lakh quantity and make it big?

It is not a big surprise that most would select the second option. For these people funding their trading account *via* collateral will not work out. No broker will provide it; can you guess why?

The option buyer is betting ₹1.1 × 16,56,000 = ₹18.22 lakh of his fund on this single trade. There is a 99% probability that he will lose all of it as the chances of Nifty climbing another 3,200 points, i.e. rising 13.6% in the following four days is rare.

No matter how practical you are, the gambler in you will likely force you to some day go with the second option. To stay rational, it's always better to select a broker who does not allow you to buy options *via* collateral. The sooner you realize that, the longer you will stay in the hunt.

You must keep in mind that in this business the broker does not have your best interest in mind. They are in the business to make money for themselves. Not just in India, anywhere in the world the banks, underwriters, financial institutions, trading agencies, investment advisors and brokerage service providers will try to squeeze the last paisa out of every deal.

There is a reason they do that. Banking is a very dangerous business to be in. Even a century or more of trust does not mean anything much; banks can still go bust in a day due to mis-management — examples are right in front of you.

Big banking institutions fail in a day, no matter the amount of fees they charge from their clients. The risks that exist in the markets today are simply unquantifiable, unmeasurable and unimaginable.

Each time the market crashes analysts do a post-mortem to determine the root cause. The academia then fixes what went wrong, only to discover years later that the new fix has broken something else.

Risk is something that you should respect and anticipate — but you need not fear it, it has nothing personal against you. It does not even know who you are!

Now, brokers have a long list of mutual funds or stocks that can be pledged, then why am I suggesting to go with debt funds?

There are two reasons for this.

Reason-1: Brokers require 50% of the funds coming from a pledged entity to be in the cash-equivalent category. This is applicable only if you carry your positions overnight.

The strategies we discussed in this book, namely credit and debit spreads, short iron condor and short iron fly can be executed by pledging shares, mutual funds, or bonds. For example, if the total margin requirement for a short iron condor is equal to ₹2 lakh, brokers will need you to maintain 50% of that, i.e. ₹1 lakh, from cash equivalent mutual funds or bonds. A few debt mutual funds and almost all government bonds including Sovereign gold bonds, are considered in the cash equivalent category.*

* Kindly check with your brokers for the list of ISINs (International Securities Identification Numbers) that belong to the cash equivalent category.

If you do not have funds in the cash equivalent category, you can still carry the position overnight but you will be charged interest for the non-cash component. Usually brokers charge from 10% to 25% interest. If we consider 18% interest to calculate, this translates into ₹4,500 interest on ₹25,000 for the year, or ₹12.30 per day.

This interest is deductible as an expense while filing income tax returns, but try to get the big picture here. Higher your collateral amount, say it is ₹20 lakh, the daily interest is approximately ₹986 per day.

On the other hand, if we keep 100% of the collateral requirement in cash-component, there is absolutely nothing to be worried about.

Reason-2: Debt funds do not depreciate, not all of them anyway. This means that your trading capital remains intact all through the year. This stability will offer you more confidence to trade in all types of market conditions.

Equity mutual funds and stocks have an unpredictable price pattern. The value of equity portfolio will go up and down. There could be a temporary dip in your portfolio value *vis-a-vis* the previous day if the stock took a beating. And had you carried positions overnight — you may even have got a margin call.

A margin call occurs when your position's actual margin requirements are higher than the collateral you have provided. If you do not respond to the margin call by adding more funds you may either get a penalty, or the broker will square off, namely close, your position without your consent.

There are many variables to fight but such a situation is not certainly the one you need to be embroiled in. Brokers squaring off positions without your consent may prove very dangerous. Firstly, they charge double the brokerage when they do so. Secondly, you might have got a better rate if you squared off your trade yourself.

The peak margin penalty could be between 1% to 10% on the amount that exceeded your collateral value. A week's earnings can get wiped out in such a margin call.

Experienced and professional traders could handle this scenario by re-adjusting their trade positions, but imagine if this situation came to you in the very first month of your trading?

Also, the debt category I recommended (GOI bonds) had an interest payout every half-year. In the last chapter we discussed how to handle running into losses; these interest payments provide you the backup capital.

Debt funds have stability while trading has uncertainty. You need to make both of them work harmoniously, just like a marriage.

The debt funds (GOI bonds) are the foundation on which we are building our trading strategies. You are free to create, edit, or modify your trading plan to suit your requirements and risk-return appetite, but you should not alter the foundation. If you make adjustments to the foundation, namely redeem or switch the debt funds (GOI bonds), you might lose stability and the trading performance may be impacted.

This also means that you cannot use just any trading style because the condition to protect your original capital will chain you to limited trading choices. That is why I said it is a marriage. In real life couples might have to settle down to raise a family, some of the high-flying career options might have to be forgone.

So, what do you want? Have a high-flying career or a stable family?

A bit of economics will help us here. Ever since human beings started trading using the barter system the basic rule has remained the same. Buy low, sell high. Merchants who have continued to prosper did that. And people who did not, went out of business.

Everything else around has changed a lot — technology, medicine, engineering, legal, travel, academics. We even have artificial Intelligence (AI) gaining traction now. Economics has not changed a bit, neither the psychology of the merchants. May be for 5,000+ years this is the only major vertical that has not seen a major overhaul.

Options trading also basically has the same logic; you should either buy low and sell high, or sell high and buy low. If you do the reverse, i.e. buy high and sell low or sell low and buy high you will lose capital. Once you lose your capital, you cannot continue in this field.

Marriage also has not changed a bit. The number one priority of a marriage continues to be the healthy upbringing of the next generation. Simon Sinek talks about the finite games and infinite games. Infinite games are those that do not have a time tag attached to it. Marriage is also an infinite game — as long as the marriage stays intact, the children get a healthy environment to grow up in and to outperform their parents.

Trading is also an infinite game. You need to stay in the hunt for as long as possible to outperform the odds stacked against you. If you play it with a short-term goal, you are not giving time enough room to work for you.

Marriage is the apt word here. That's because each couple is different in real life. It's like in chemistry; two elements combine to become a compound, and this compound has totally different characteristics than the combining elements.

Take the example of water; it's made of hydrogen and oxygen, both of which fire friendly whereas water is its chief enemy.

My specific point is that your trading strategy and the pledge amount handling should be unique to you. Your competitor should be you, there is no point in comparing your strategy or profits or competency with another trader. This is not college where the first comer gets a medal. In real life, there are no medals and no scoring system — staying alive and in the fray in itself is the biggest reward.

The strategies that I use have not changed over the years, and I have tried my best to keep them as simple as possible. There are two elements to my trading strategy:

1. A directional strategy. Wherein I carry overnight.
2. A non-directional strategy that is deployed intraday.

If the markets are trending, my directional strategy will perform well, and the non-directional strategy will run into losses. If the markets are not moving, then the directional strategy does not punch any orders, but the non-directional strategy will generate profits.

Determining which strategy to use and which one not to is the toughest part for which I usually rely on technical analysis to decide what to do.

1. If the index has just broken out from a resistance level, I usually give more weightage to the directional strategy and that too on the bullish side.
2. If the index is stuck between a support and a resistance zone, I will make use of the non-directional strategy.
3. If the index has broken down from a support level then the directional strategy towards the bearish side will be prioritized.

There are plenty of social media influencers who are selling a course, and trading strategies to make money. You might then ask, am I not doing the same thing by selling this book? In fact, I do not know how much money I would get by publishing this book. I just love writing and was fascinated by it from 2008. I thought of compiling my three years of my hard work into something that could be of use to others. If the book sells, I am glad the information is getting passed on. Of course, I would not mind the extra money that might come in as well.

I maintain a trading diary that's publicly viewable — the daily price moves, any unusual patterns or anomaly which catches my attention get mentioned in it. The content, research and charts are all free of cost. I blog daily on https://viswaram.com/

To summarize this chapter: how you handle trading based on collateral from pledged debt funds is what really matters. Never ever take shortcuts or get carried away when someone tells you there is another guaranteed way to make money in stock markets.

You might be yearning to generate profits. Maybe you have done the hard work consistently for many weeks but are still unable to generate profits. That is usually when you get desperate, believe an influencer or stranger, and fall for their "100% guaranteed trading strategies" software or courses. The best thing to do is to remain cool, have faith in your skills, and do the necessary hard work. Things will then work out for the good.

Since trading is an individual activity, we may have additional pressure to perform. Sometimes when you look at other traders posting fancy profit screenshots on social media — you might really lose your cool and fall for the first shortcut that is available.

This is where you need to keep your mind calm. Any profitable trading setup will take time to build. There are no shortcuts. It is both essential and really beneficial if you put the efforts to build it step by step without expecting an immediate return.

Always remember, till your trading system is perfected you have those debt funds working round the clock to provide you passive income. Use that safety net to your advantage and focus on building your trading strategy perfectly!

17

~

Simple and Humble Daily Returns

THE EASIEST WAY TO STAY HAPPY is to be simple. Lower your expectations for a while, and focus on getting things done.

Earning 8% to 12% returns a year translates to 0.66% to 1% return per month. This was the ceiling of my expectation when I began. Many people, however, come to the stock market wanting to make 50% to 80% returns a year — that's where the problem comes in.

I am not asking you to lower your ambition or kill your dream of becoming wealthy. I am just asking you to keep it under control till the mission of becoming knowledgeable is accomplished. To start with, let learning get higher priority over earning.

It's possible that the first trade you took gave you outsized returns. You might have even had a winning spree in the first few months. That may well have been due to beginner's luck. Trust me when I say trading is a tough job, and to keep generating profits month on month is stressful.

If your return expectations are unrealistically high, it may create unwanted pressure on you to overtrade. The easiest solution is to first lower your expectations, then create a working strategy, and then gain the confidence to scale up with a larger capital.

Look for trades that have a higher probability of profit with respect to your risk profile, your capital and where the timing is right even though the profit amount is lower. This will set the ball rolling in a favorable direction.

To make 1% on your trading capital you need to make ₹18,000 per month. As matters stand, this is about the entry level salary in some of the IT firms, banks and services sector. So, 18K is not a bad amount!

To make ₹18,000 from 20 trading days in a month, you need to make ₹900 per day. Let us start there.

Making ₹900 per day is not the priority, but finding a trading opportunity that can deliver ₹900 is. Probably you did not understand this — so let me elaborate.

If you start the day with the plan to make ₹900, then your brain will laser focus to find an opportunity that can do that for you. Out of all the option strikes you are watching, maybe the right one will reveal itself to you.

For example, you find an options contract (strike) quoting for ₹100 and you order 100 quantity of it. The total order value will be ₹10,000 (₹100 × 100 qty). To generate a profit of ₹900, the strike has to appreciate to ₹109 (₹9 × 100 qty). If for some reason, you sense that the strike will not go to ₹109, you may even decide to book profits prematurely, say at ₹105 (₹5 × 100 qty) = ₹500. According to me, booking a profit of ₹500 instead of the expected ₹900 is still a win. Had you held on to the same strike, you could have gone into a deeper loss.

The important aspect is to get your entry and exit right. In options trading there could be a lot of variables at play and something nasty could turn up any time during the trade. Sometimes this strike may quickly drop to ₹96 — that's when your stop loss should be ready to catch you from losing big.

In the above example, ₹900 was the theoretical maximum that could have been achieved and we extracted 55.55% of the maximum profits out of it — it's a good start. Nobody has gone bankrupt by taking small profits!

There is no compulsion to stay in a trade in order to try and get the maximum possible value from it. You can exit when you feel it's comfortable and safe. In my trading journey I have seen a profitable position turn into loss due to my over confidence. I have also seen a position becoming profitable after I exited it. Nobody can predict these things very accurately — we are always working on probabilities.

By choosing smaller targets you also relieve a lot of pressure to outperform the benchmark. And this will enable you to gather enough courage to believe in your strategy and achieve your trading goals.

Once you get comfortable, it is then okay to flex your muscles and set higher goals. Goals that will push you to peak performance.

In real life there will be someone to push us, our family or a friend or a boss. Even though it may feel irritating, that push could propel us to achieve something big, like a college degree, a job or a promotion.

In trading there is nobody to do that. Even if you consult your spouse or friend, they might have no idea about what you are doing. Trading is a difficult business to explain to others; particularly as most of them might think it is gambling.

Here you must be your own boss, and you need to change gears and step on the accelerator when required. When you win you need to win big so that you can save money. There will be periods of loss, too — so these savings will see you through.

And, lastly, there is nothing really to brag about. After all, trading is just another job. Sometimes I see people posting their P/L on social media. I think it's totally unnecessary.

Have you seen a surgeon posting his surgery fee on social media. Or, a lawyer displaying his fee. An architect showing his consultation fees. Trading, too is just another job from making money.

Well, if you have created a big dent in the world — there is nothing wrong in showing off. I am quite sure Mr. Soros would have posted on social media how he shorted the GBP and made a fortune in 1992 if it were available back then. Occasionally, you can see some fascinating trades like these and those traders take the limelight.

Visibility of Profits When Buying and Selling Options

Options buying has a higher profit potential compared to options selling. The reason is pure mathematics; let me explain.

Option buying has limited downside risk — limited to the premium paid — but unlimited upside potential. On the other hand, option selling offers only limited profits — limited to the premium received — but potentially unlimited downside risk.

For example, let us consider the two parties in an options transaction, one is the option buyer and the other the option seller.

- If the market is moving in his direction and he wishes to close the trade, the buyer makes profit, and the seller's pocket is emptied.
- If the option expires worthless, on the other hand, then the option seller would get to keep the entire premium paid by the option buyer.

The visibility on how much profits can be made is the real deal, and that is where most traders go wrong. They may be 100% correct about the market's direction, timing, etc. Still they would not really know how much profit can be extracted from the market at the time of buying an option.

Option selling comes with an in-built visibility. The seller knows how much his maximum earnings will be. But the seller would have no idea about how much maximum losses he could run into.

When an option contract is made, it has a buyer and a seller. At any point in time, only one of them makes money. The amount of money a buyer makes is the same as the money the seller loses (excluding the brokerage and charges). Depending on market conditions, the time to expiry, and volatility, you should decide whether buying or selling options is the right strategy.

Since we are trading weekly expiries, there are ample opportunities to become an option seller or an option buyer. If you prefer intraday trading, being an option seller will even give you control on the maximum loss which could be set by a stop loss order.

To be successful in options buying, you need to get both the direction and the speed of price movement absolutely correct. If the market starts picking up momentum, the options you have bought could even go in the money very quickly, doubling or quadrupling the premium your paid. This is usually when greed kicks in and we wish to stay in the trade to extract even more profits. And more often we end up not booking profits at all.

It is a good idea to put down in writing the returns you wish to extract from reach trade. For example, you could set a return of 100% on the option premium paid and exit the trade once that level has reached.

Do not get me wrong; I mean 100% ROI not on your capital but on the premium paid. For example, let's say Nifty is at 23700 and the 24100 CE has a price of ₹10 with four days left to expiry. Now if Nifty makes an intraday up move of 1%, then there is a high likelihood that 24100 CE premium will surge to ₹25. You would then have made ₹375 (15 × 25) per lot on this trade.

And it would not be a bad idea to book profits at that time because we never know if Nifty will retrace the gains or move full steam ahead. If it moves ahead, we may miss out on future gains, but if it falls or stays flat — the premium of ₹25 will start eroding due to time decay.

In options trading the maximum money is made when an option strike starts as an OTM and then goes ITM. The returns in percentage will be enormous. If you feel something like that is going to happen, then it is the right time to put on the option buyer's hat. This does not happen every week; we may need a break out or break down trade for this to happen. Even a strong news flow could do this. Breakouts and breakdowns could be guessed with a certain level of accuracy using technical analysis, but there is no way to forecast or plan for news events.

The broader point I am trying to make here is the need to have clear visibility on how much profit you should take in every trade. Let it be simple and humble.

During your first three years in the market, do not let greed cloud your decision making. Small profits over multiple trades are way better than one big profit in a year, both psychologically and financially.

~

Section

~

6

18

~

Scaling Up and Up

ONCE YOU ARE CONFIDENT OF YOUR EDGE and your trading plan, it is just a matter of time before the floodgates of money open for you. It will not happen easily since an edge is the most difficult thing to achieve.

Edge is something that gives you a specific advantage for making money. It is not an illegal or illegitimate thing such as insider trading. Instead, it could even be a mathematical model that gives you a buy/sell signal before the general public sees it.

Let it be said that we are not talking here about making money *via* insider trading, corruption, or though political advantage. Even if you make money that way — it will not last as you are still financially illiterate. Since you don't have the financial skill set you will end up giving back the money to the market. It's like someone who wins the lottery; however big the amount is, he will eventually lose it all.

Financial literacy is best acquired step-by-step. If you rush into it, you will miss many a key lesson. Ideally, financial concepts, trades, investing, financial instruments, etc. should be taught at school.

Coming back to the edge part — it is that magical elixir you need to discover. And, your edge is specific to you. It's not a generalized utility.

Even if you copy another successful trader, there is no guarantee that both of you will get similar results. The reason is the mindset — s/he might have a difference perception of risk and you might have the opposite. It's best that you design your own trading plan and refrain from copying other traders.

There is nothing wrong with having a directional view. Your research and analysis may tell you that the market is bearish while others could have a contrarian bullish view. You should have the courage and faith to follow your research and not dilly-dally based on other opinions or views. You just need to remember that you need to cut your losses if the market proves you wrong — and enjoy the profits if the market is going in your direction.

Always remember there should be someone with the opposite view from yours to complete the trade. If everyone were a bull, then nobody will sell. And if everyone were a bear then there will be no buyers.

In Chapter 13 we discussed backtests and win rates. We also learnt that even having a win percentage just above 50% would work out in our favor if we adjust the risk-return ratio to 1:2. After multiple tests, combinations, and permutations if you can bring this win rate above 68.2%, you might have discovered that sweet spot. It may take you many weeks or months to fine-tune your strategies to achieve this win rate, but rest assured that this effort will pay off.

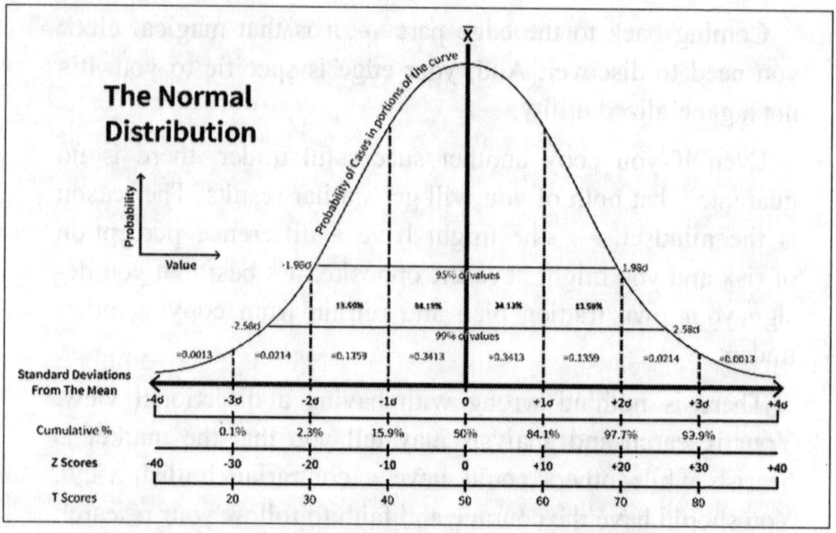

Figure 18.1: **Normal Distribution Curve (Bell Curve)**

~

68.2% has a lot of significance in options trading; let's see how. Figure 17.1 illustrates a normal distribution curve, also called a bell curve, that plots the probability of an event occurring. If Nifty is plotted at the Y-axis, i.e. at the 0 (zero) level, then the probability that it will stay between +1σ and -1σ = 68.2% i.e. 34.13% × 2. And the probability that it will stay between +2σ and -2σ = 95% i.e. (34.13+13.59) × 2. Sigma (σ), is called the standard deviation.

If a mathematician analyses the options trade data, then sigma shows the level of confidence, or probability, of an event occurring. In other words, he would say he has a 68.2% confidence level that Nifty will stay between +1σ and -1σ over the next week, and a 95% confidence that it stays between +2σ and -2σ. Every option trading software provides the values of +1σ, +2σ, and +3σ, and it is highly recommended to use this data to design your strategies.

The above paragraphs may seem pretty hard to understand for starters, but I urge you to look up probability theory online. Professional traders prefer options trading because its roots are based on probability. They get some comfort when the odds are in their favor. Just imagine, if someone told you the chances of winning an event are 30%, 50%, and 68.2% respectively, which would you choose? I am quite sure, I will go with the 68.2% event.

I recommend you revisit the above paragraphs once you have googled about standard deviations, the probability of profit and the bell curve. I am simply highlighting the fact that option trading has a lot to do with probability and you should be able to use that to your advantage.

> **Important:** These are just mathematical probabilities and in an actual scenario, Nifty could exceed 1σ, 2σ, or even 3σ in a week. Bottom line: your strategies should be able to limit the losses if the trade does not go the way you planned for.

There is no way you can generate profits all the time. Firstly, because there are slippages in actual trading *vis-à-vis* backtests. Backtests rely on historical data, whereas live trading uses values that change every tick. Typically, live trading will give poorer results than do backtests, and not the other way round.

Secondly, in real life trading you lose money in brokerage, transaction charges, stamp duty, and taxes. Thirdly, the major volumes come from institutional desks, they have a better talent pool, faster computers, and smarter algorithms, and there is no way to beat them all the time. If there were higher probability strategies, they would use them and ensured the arbitrage opportunities were no more available.

Even if you create and execute a high-performance strategy, there could be times when you become complacent and stop pushing your limits. This is where you need to pull yourself up and stay alert in the game. Hitherto successful strategies could stop working one fine day due to changes in market structures, sentiment or some other reasons, and you should not be out of ideas when that happens. There could also be periods of lower volatility, lower volumes, or lesser speculation. This may translate into lower earnings as the options premium will be lower at such times. This is where you also need a bit of optimism and hope.

You need to believe that markets will present an opportunity the next day, even if there isn't any today. Hoping for good market conditions tomorrow will keep you out of unnecessary trades today.

Making money should not excite you. Instead, the processes and systems that you create to make money should. How you make the money is the most important thing — it should come *via* skill not luck.

I have heard people say that anyone can become a successful trader. I do not agree. In options trading you need some special skill sets — only if you are educated, have a math background and know computer skills will you be able to generate money.

Anyone could make money from stock markets. Indeed, there are many multi-millionaires who bought a stock and then simply forgot to sell it. There are no similar stories about option trading so far. That's because option trading requires active management and lightning quick reflexes.

Once you have found your elixir (edge) you can replicate it on other stocks or indices and multiply your earning potential. People don't trade just equities these days; they also trade commodities, currencies, etc. as well. Then there are people who trade on international markets, although that's quite difficult to do from India.

What Do You Do With the Money Coming in?

Debt funds have not outperformed the equity markets if the time frame considered is more than 10 years. The outperformance comes only from equity.

To create massive wealth, debt mutual funds will not be enough. You need to have equity exposure, either directly by investing in high-quality stocks or selecting good mutual funds. The only reason we have kept the initial capital in the debt funds category (GOI Bonds) is to provide a stable platform for trading. But this does not mean you need to prioritize investing in debt over equity for additional investments.

Meanwhile, you can use the extra time to become a small research analyst for yourself and your family. I know SEBI restricts analysts who have not registered with them. Your research is for you, only when you post your recommendations to someone would it become an issue. There is no harm in being your own research analyst.

You can consider making time to hunt for quality multibagger ideas to invest in it. If you do not prefer to do your own stock picking research — then you can invest in stocks *via* some good mutual funds that have a lower expense ratio.

Maintaining a high performance level is the hardest thing. Every high performer, whether it be an athlete, an artist, an expert will go through ups and downs. Maintaining humility when you are hitting your highs and sustaining your hopes high during your down levels should help you cruise through.

Trading may perhaps be the only business that gives you money on individual merit. Everywhere else there is politics and uncertainty. Let me explain.

Even if you are a talented cricketer it's not easy to get into the India's national playing eleven. There are a lot of things that you have to do and know lots of people, etc. in order to make it. Being in the top 1% will still not cut it, you need to be in the playing eleven from among all the competing players — the hardest thing to do.

If you are an excellent automobile mechanic still you won't get assured returns every month. You may have to open your own garage somewhere and people should see someone else bring their vehicle in first. It could take a lot of time before you taste success.

If you are an excellent employee the chance of getting promoted, or being in the top 5%, is always doubtful. Your performance also depends on how you treat other people and how other people like you. First, there should be a vacancy for you to be promoted. You might also require a basket of "getting liked by other people" skills along with your "core competency." There may be office politics involved and you may be victim of it directly or indirectly.

If you are an entrepreneur and also have an excellent idea you might still not be successful. Even if things go your way, the government could impose a lockdown and bankrupt you. The tax rules or import/export rules could change and jeopardize your progress. Even labor rules or unionization of workers could be a threat.

You can think of various other fields and fill in the blanks for yourself. In trading you just need a computer, an internet connection, electricity and a good broker. The amount of money you make is directly proportional to your own skills and efforts. Unless the government comes with some unexplainable reforms you can continue doing your work from a place that suits your work profile.

Personally I did not come into trading to make big money or earn a name. Covid lockdown had almost shuttered my clothing business and I had to find funds to continue paying the staff, rentals and other recurring costs.

All I had were some mutual funds that were SIP funded from 2007 to 2015. So I could not touch that as this was my safety net. This brought me to the only option — to learn trading by using this accumulated fund as collateral. I learnt from brokers that they needed a 50% cash equivalent but the mutual funds I had were not eligible. So I redeemed everything and moved into liquid funds and money market funds.

I had to find money consistently every month to pay the dues. I could not run into losses any single month as it would impact the recurring debt payments of my other business.

At the end of three years I was able to make just enough money to pay the creditors from the other business, and when I sat down and calculated the returns it was over 16% every single year!

~

19

~

Monitoring Your Trading Returns Every Month

MONITORING YOUR PROFIT AND LOSS regularly is an important but often omitted step. The best advice here is to maintain a trading journal.

The things that should go into the journal are:

1. Each trade you took;
2. The positions you are holding overnight;
3. MTM or profit/loss booked;
4. The time and quantity of orders;
5. The rationale of why you took each trade;
6. Did the trading go as per your original plan (Y/N);
7. Did you fire fight your existing position with a new position (Y/N).

It also makes sense to pen down your emotion, or any unusual patterns you saw during the day. Even if you did not take a trade, record what you saw on the charts. If you took a holiday / leave, then ignore that day's entry.

Points 1 to 4 can usually be downloaded in a csv or Excel sheet format as provided by the broker. If the broker does not provide it, you might have to manually create it.

Points 5 to 7 are your version of the story. In fact, this is going to be the major difference in your next three years. When you start noting down your trading execution the entire system gets cemented in your brain.

This is the best feedback / validation you can achieve for your work. Most of us do not have the luxury to work under a great mentor or at a great company that punches billions of trades every month. An individual trader has some limitations, so you can try this method for feedback and self-improvement.

When I started documenting my trades, I had no clue about the benefit of doing so. Since I loved writing, I kept elaborate explanations of how my trading went by. This improved my analytical ability over time.

In the monthly review there are two things that must be separately accounted for:

1. Trading profits/loss;
2. Interest income/appreciation from the debt funds.

Trading profit / loss is the result of what you do, while interest income is what the money achieves for you. One is active and the other passive.

It will be nice to be able to have a profitable month, but it need not always be that way. You need to be a genius to report profits from the very first day. Typically, we must wait patiently till our edge gets going.

Once you monitor three months in succession, you will have a fair idea whether you are improving or not. If you are going backwards then it's a good time to add to your knowledge *via* books, podcasts, technical classes or coaching.

If you have no failure in three months then that is also a worrying aspect. That is because failures etch our memory with the exact reasons which is of immense help when a trade goes in the similar fashion next time.

For example, if your stop loss got hit and you took a loss — that conditioning will remain in your mind for some time. This drives you to do further research and to rework the strategy next time.

You are still not able to make it even after a year then it is better to try something else. No, I am not discouraging you but this field is very difficult and only the elite 5% make it. It is always good to have the realization that you are not cut out for this. It will also help you find another field of interest.

However, if you can make good progress *via* learning as well as earning then you should hang on. Time will correct your mistakes by providing you ample opportunity every week.

Remember, only 5% of traders make it, if you are one of them — then your time ahead is going to be awesome!

Just like you monitor your profit/loss, it is also good to monitor your health and well-being. Since trading is stressful, it could have a major health impact. This stress is mostly felt in the early years as there is high uncertainty. Sometimes you will not even know if you are stressed, you might need additional help. Once you become a seasoned professional, your stress levels will drastically come down.

~

20

~

How to Join the Top 1% Options Traders Club

UNTIL 2023 INDIAN MARKETS had only one expiry day every week, namely Thursdays. Thus, both Nifty50 and BankNifty indices had weekly expiries on Thursdays. If a Thursday fell on a public holiday, the expiry would be on the preceding day.

After the Covid lockdown in 2020, there was big growth in the number of traders flocking to the stock market, not just in India but worldwide. As speculation volumes grew, the market institutions opened up newer avenues for the traders to speculate. One such decision was to launch 0DTE (Zero Day to Expiry) in the US markets. Indian markets adapted to a similar version by having an expiry day every working day.

NSE started the trend by introducing FinNifty (Nifty Financial Services Index) expiring on Tuesdays, Midcap Select expiries on Mondays, and moving BankNifty expiry to Wednesdays instead of Thursdays. BSE also introduced its own index expiries for Sensex which expired on Fridays and Bankex expiring on Mondays.

Expiry trading, i.e. intraday trading on expiry days, picked up momentum and more and more new and inexperienced traders got pulled into this system, eventually turning trading into more of a gambling game. These newer traders started approaching options trading as a hero-to-zero sport, just like a lottery, and most of them would end up losing their hard-earned capital.

The exchanges even had plans to introduce extra trading hours from 6 p.m. to 9 p.m. so that office goers could participate in trading activities after they returned home from work.

SEBI published a consultation paper dated 30 July 2024 which highlighted that derivative turnover (futures and options contracts) had surpassed cash market turnover manifold (*see* Table 20.1).* This report also highlighted that expiry day speculation was at dangerously high levels.

On 1 October 2024, SEBI issued another new circular titled "Measures to Strengthen Equity Index Derivatives Framework for Increased Investor Protection and Market Stability".**

In this circular, SEBI directed the exchanges to limit weekly expiries to just one index. SEBI also mandated increasing the contract size from ₹5 to less 10 lakh to ₹15 to 20 lakh effective from 20 November 2024. Even for option buyers, effective 1 February 2025, SEBI also asked trading members (brokers) to increase the Initial Margin (IM) and Extreme Loss Margin (ELM).

---

* Source: https://www.sebi.gov.in/reports-and-statistics/reports/jul-2024/consultation-paper-on-measures-to-strengthen-index-derivatives-framework-for-increased-investor-protection-and-market-stability_85279.html

** Source: https://www.sebi.gov.in/legal/circulars/oct-2024/measures-to-strengthen-equity-index-derivatives-framework-for-increased-investor-protection-and-market-stability_87208.html

Table 20.1

Trend in Annual Turnover in F&O Segment

Turnover – Market wide (in ₹ Lakh Cr.)	*FY18*	*FY19*	*FY20*	*FY21*	*FY22*	*FY23*	*FY24*
Index Futures	48.0	55.5	67.0	90.5	84.5	95.0	74.0
Stock Futures	156.0	161.5	148.5	181.0	210.5	190.5	255.5
Index Options (Premium)	4.5	6.5	11.0	26.5	58.5	109.5	138.0
Stock Options (Premium)	1.5	2.0	2.5	6.0	10.5	9.5	14.0
Total Turnover (Premium)	210.0	225.5	228.5	303.5	363.5	405.0	481.5
Notional Turnover	1,650	2,376	3,445	6,436	16,952	38,223	79,927
Turnover in Cash Market	83.2	87.2	96.6	164.4	179.1	143.3	217.3
Ratio of F&O Turnover (Premium) to Cash Turnover	2.5	2.6	2.4	1.8	2.0	2.8	2.2
Ratio of F&O Turnover (Notional) to Cash Market Turnover	19.8	27.2	35.7	39.1	94.7	266.7	367.8
Nifty 50 Index 31 March	10,211.8	11,623.9	8,597.8	14,690.7	17,464.8	17,359.8	22,326.9

Finally, SEBI decided to increase the ELM for short options contracts by 2% on expiry day. Suppose the margin requirement for selling 1 lot of 23400 CE position was ₹70,000 rupees, an additional 2% charge will be approximately ₹23400 × 25 (lot size) × 2% = ₹11,700. So the revised margin requirements will be ₹70,000 + ₹11,700 = ₹81,700. If NSE decides to change the lot size, you might have to calculate the new margin requirements accordingly.

Handling Changes in Regulations and Reforms

If you wish to become a full-time trader you need to be aware that the trading structure, rules and regulations do not remain constant forever. You must always remember that regulators, exchanges, and brokers can come up with a new set of rules that may jeopardize your trading system. Even a small increase in brokerage costs could vender your trading system unviable. Also, the Government can come up with new taxation rules at any time, rules that could severely dent your earnings and profits.

You need to provide sufficient leeway in your trading plan to accommodate such changes. For example, a change in contract size could mean your current trading algorithm may not work tomorrow — you may have to reconfigure it. Similarly, if the margin requirements go up, newbie traders may find it difficult to trade and this could suck out the liquidity from the markets — leading to higher slippage costs than usual.

The best way to handle these changes is by staying humble and setting reasonable return expectations in the beginning. You must also stay lean so that you can make room for changes as and when they occur. Also, keep innovating and never assume you have found a permanent magic formula to make money which would ever require any change.

As you perfect your trading system and gain confidence you can try out multiple trading strategies, styles and techniques.

Handling Changes in the Index or the Underlying

The concepts discussed in this book are about Nifty which is the preferred index among professional traders. Tomorrow the dynamics could change and some other index may become the bellwether for professional traders. This does not mean that the ideas and strategies discussed in this book will become dated.

Even though the trading ideas discussed in this chapter are based on Nifty, the same strategies will work on Sensex or any of the popular indices anywhere in the world. All you need to know is the strike intervals and the lot sizes. For example, Nifty has a strike interval of 50 points and the lot size is 25. Sensex has a strike interval of 100 points and the lot size is 10. For new contracts created after 21st November 2024, the lot size of Nifty would be 75 and Sensex would be 20, the strike intervals of 50 and 100 points each stays unchanged.

Based on these two pieces of information you can recalculate the maximum profit and maximum losses on each of the strategies discussed above.

In case you are not sure how to do the calculations yourself, you can use the free online calculator provided by Opstra DefineEdge or Sensibull.

Manual Trading *versus* Automated Trading

Once you are profitable as a discretionary trader using manual trading, you can start automating and become a systems trader. The advantage of being a systems trader is that it takes your emotions out of the picture.

When you are automating things, namely creating an algorithm for computerized trading. Remember, that no trading system in the world has 100% accuracy. There will be losing days as well as winning days. I am here to reassure you that it is okay to lose, just so long as you can keep the losses small so that you can continue in this journey.

Selection of Trading Strategies

Try to stick with the trading strategies described in this book for the first three years, namely:

1. Debit / Credit Spread.
2. Short / Long Iron Fly.
3. Short / Long Iron Condors.

These three strategies are limited-profit and limited-loss strategies. Your earnings and losses are pre-defined and capped ensuring you do not run into a huge or unanticipated loss which could wipe out your capital. With practice, you will get better and you could then try out complicated strategies, or even invent something on your own.

Use of Emergency Funds

In Chapter 14 we discussed how much ledger balance you ought to maintain. Roughly, you need to keep 2% of your total capital as cash balance to be used for emergencies. Also, this should be the maximum permitted loss you can incur over four months. Once your losses exceed this pre-defined target, you should take a break till your interest income from the GOI bonds can again top-up your ledger balance.

I request you to abide by this rule during the initial three years because the bulk of the money lost by traders is not in the initial trade but in counter trades, i.e. "revenge trades" done after a losing trade in the hope of recovering those losses. Professional traders never go in for revenge trading, so its advisable for a newcomer to stay out of it; take a trading break instead is the next best option.

Backtest, Backtest and Forward Test

The secret to high performance trading boils down to knowledge. The easiest way to acquire such knowledge is to mine and analyze historical data. Backtesting is nothing but finding instances in the past where your trading strategy worked out well or poorly; and then deploying similar trades when those kinds of situations reappear. Luckily, testing on historical data sets is not that costly and you should seriously consider devoting sufficient time for this research.

We talked about forward testing in Chapter 13. It is a process where you simulate your strategy for the next 3 to 6 months before trading with real money. The only drawback in this process is that you need to wait for some time before the results appear. But this strategy will work is perfect for a newcomer as you do not go through the pain of losing money while learning.

Sticking to the Plan

The only way to beat fixed deposit returns and enter that 1% category is to use the margin pledge option discussed in

Chapter 6. The magic that works in your favor is that your money continues to earn fixed deposit equivalent returns even if you are struggling with trading in the initial months.

When you pledge debt funds or GOI bonds you remain the owner of the funds and continue to get their interest income. And because you used the pledge feature provided by your broker and exchange, you need not bring in fresh capital to trade.

You just need to stick to the plan and run on a tight leash till you discover your own edge. Even if you discover a profitable path toward the end of the second year, you can still come out on top.

Trading Options *versus* Trading Stocks

There are people who trade options and then there are others who trade stocks. What I have observed is that if the capital is either too low or too high people end up trading stocks. And people with mid-range capital seem to prefer trading options.

There are two or three variables at play here:

1. If your capital is very low, you would need a big percentage win to raise it. So an investing kind of mindset will work out well. Let us assume you have a capital of ₹1 lakh, and you invest it in a stock XYZ. After three months if XYZ goes up by 25%, your new capital becomes ₹1.25 lakh. There are tons of stocks that go up 25% in a quarter, or even 100% a year. Of course, it may take days of research to find the ones that can do so. Is it worth making this effort? It really depends on your risk profile.

2. If your capital is very huge, say above ₹100 crore — it's highly recommended that you stick with stocks. Portfolio managers, mutual fund managers, hedge funds handle huge capital in equity markets. Most of them are highly skilled and talented and they will be able to find high return stocks very easily. Also they will not plan to take a trade everyday — once or twice a month is good enough. Further, these people trade only stocks since futures and options come with a risk element and the trading frequency is also higher. Also every time they buy a stock, they have the luxury to buy adequate quantity to make a difference in the ROI.
3. For all those falling in between, options trading provides the benefit of leverage. From a mindset perspective these people are highly ambitious and ready to take some risks to increase their capital.

Handling Stress

Watching your trading positions go in the red and your capital diminishing is the most stressful state in trading. People could go crazy or even have a heart-attack — and this has happened many times in real life.

Only those people who can keep their heads cool can make it in the long run. So if it's not the right field for you, get to know that as early as possible to save your time.

And if you can handle this kind of stress, then trading is going to work miracles for you.

~

I sincerely hope that this book has shown you a path on how to be in the top 1% and beating the level of fixed deposit returns in the first three years. This book shown you that path, the decision to make the journey is all yours.

~

21

~

Enjoying Your Trading Days Ahead!

IF YOU HAVE REACHED TILL HERE, it means that you now have all the basic information necessary to consider launching your trading career.

Is it going to be a smooth and fast ride? Absolutely not.

Is it going to be exciting and challenging? Absolutely yes.

As I said earlier, trading is a job — respect it, value it and nurture it. It will give you more than 100x returns on time, effort and money in due course.

I have read of many people getting fired from their jobs, but I've never read about a top-performer getting laid off. Similarly, if you are at the top of your trading profession there is nothing to be worried. If you get lazy, complacent, or overconfident the markets will take away more than it gave you.

For a sub-par performer, the markets can be a brutal place. And I personally do not recommend anyone to take up a career in trading if they are not willing to upgrade their math, computational ability and upskill their financial literacy.

If you have dedicated yourself to becoming the best in this field, nothing can stop you. As it stands no social, economic, political, legal or environmental reforms will restrict you from trading in stock markets.

Unless the government bans stock trading or speculation completely, or if SEBI bans the usage of margin pledge for trading activity, I do not see any hindrance that could come in your way.

Compare this with a regular corporate job where even a ₹1 increase in fuel prices will impact your travel expense. The employer could extend your working hours, or not give you a pay raise. They could even transfer you to another location. Office politics could be stressful and career hampering. Your boss could restrict your holidays or even give you a lower rating during appraisals.

Your trading job on the other hand is not dependent on these factors. You just need a computer, internet, electricity and a brokerage account to enable you to trade. Your cost of doing business does not rise unless the internet or electricity expenses rise. You need not travel for work; you need not even buy brand new clothes every year. And the exact working hours will be from 09.15 a.m. to 15.30 p.m., five days a week.

Your performance and payouts largely depend on your individual merit. Your income will rise in proportion to the financial knowledge you acquire. You do not have to convince or persuade anyone else to give you a better rating or appraisal. Also, you can switch off the computer and take a day off at your own discretion.

So, what would you decide to be?

Thank you for reading my work and I look forward to your support going forward. I hope this book has opened your eyes and ears to a new dimension.

All the best!

References and Further Reading

- Achelis, Steven B.: *Technical Analysis from A to Z.*
- Augen, Jeff: *Trading Options at Expiration: Strategies and Models for Winning the Endgame.*
- Benklifa, Michael: *Think Like an Option Trader: How to Profit by Moving from Stocks to Options.*
- Caplan, David L.: *The New Option Secret — Volatility: The Weapon of the Professional Trader and the Most Important Indicator in Option Trading.*
- Chen, Dennis A. and Sebastian, Mark: *The Option Traders Hedge Fund.*
- Cohen, Guy: *Options Made Easy: Your Guide to Profitable Trading.*
- Cohen, Guy: *The Bible of Options Strategies: The Definitive Guide for Practical Trading Strategies.*
- Cohen, Guy: *Volatile Markets Made Easy: Trading Stocks and Options for Increased Profits.*
- Cordier, James and Gross, Michael: *The Complete Guide to Option Selling.*
- Couling, Anna: *A Complete Guide to Volume Price Analysis.*
- Elder, Alexander: *Trading for a Living.*

— Fischer, Jens and Fischer, Robert: *Candlesticks, Fibonacci and Chart Pattern Trading Tools: A Synergistic Strategy to Enhance Profits and Reduce Risk.*
— Friedentag, Harvey C.: *The Stock Option Income Generator: How To Make Steady Profits by Renting Your Stocks.*
— Housel, Morgan: *The Psychology of Money.*
— Lefevre, Edwin: *Reminiscences of a Stock Operator.*
— Lowell, Lee: *Get Rich with Options: Four Winning Strategies Straight from the Exchange Floor.*
— McMillan, Lawrence: *Profit with Options: Essential Methods for Investing.*
— Morales, Gil and Kacher, Chris: *Short-Selling with the O'Neil Disciples: Turn to the Dark Side of Trading.*
— Murphy, John J.: *Intermarket Technical Analysis.*
— Murphy, John J.: *Technical Analysis of the Financial Markets: A Comprehensive Guide to Trading Methods and Applications.*
— Nations, Scott: *The Complete Book of Option Spreads and Combinations: Strategies for Income Generation, Directional Moves, and Risk Reduction.*
— Passarelli, Dan: *Trading Options Greeks: How Time, Volatility, and Other Pricing Factors Drive Profits.*
— Person, JL: *Mastering the Stock Market — High Probability Market Timing and Stock Selection Tools.*
— Pring, Martin J.: *Technical Analysis Explained, Fifth Edition: The Successful Investor's Guide to Spotting Investment Trends and Turning Points.*
— Schwager, Jack D.: *Market Wizards* (all books).
— Sinclair, Euan: *Volatility Trading.*